"In *Can You Keep Your Faith* [ ] a
need that has been ignored for [ ] y
high school senior and college freshman should read this book."

—ANDY STANLEY
Senior Pastor, North Point Community Church

"*Can You Keep Your Faith in College?* explores the difficult times
college students face as they enter a new world away from the
influence of their home and church. *Can You Keep Your Faith
in College?* shares the experiences of college students and how
they faced the challenges and temptations of life on campus.
Young people going off to college or already in the midst of
their college life will gain great insight and wisdom from reading these real-life incidents and how students of faith handled
some difficult times. Abbie Smith has utilized her experience
and been open in sharing the truths in a manner that will help
students to better face the opportunities, trials, and experiences
of everyday college pressure and life."

—DAL SHEALY
President/CEO, Fellowship of Christian Athletes

"This is an excellent book…down to earth, focused, and real. It
is also a fun book to read. It provides practical help from col-
lege-aged men and women who are in the process of
experiencing the vital issues of life and faith."

—JERRY E. WHITE, PhD
President, The Navigators
Author of *Making the Grade: A Guide to Excellence in College*

"What will a Christian at a secular college have to deal with? The students who speak in this book will tell you, fresh from the experiences that molded them. They talk frankly about dorm life, peer pressure, academics, and dating. They tell about how they found fellowship, developed habits of obedience, learned to minister and lead—all in a culture that at first seemed antithetical to all they believed. These are real voices telling of their struggles and successes in the first person. They give a vivid picture of what it means to be a witnessing community on campus. Abbie Smith has done a great service for high school students, parents, and guidance counselors by letting us hear directly from students who walk the campus world by faith."

—ALEC HILL
President, InterVarsity Christian Fellowship

"*Can You Keep Your Faith in College?* is a brilliant idea for a book and a huge challenge for any believer in the university scene. I love Abbie Smith's vision for this resource and believe students are going to be encouraged and challenged by the stories of God's faithfulness from campuses across the nation."

—LOUIE GIGLIO
Passion Conferences

ABBIE SMITH

CAN**YOU**KEEP **YOUR**FAITH ᴵᴺCOLLEGE?

Multnomah Books

CAN YOU KEEP YOUR FAITH IN COLLEGE?
published by Multnomah Books
a division of Random House, Inc.
Published in association with VMI Publishers-Agency
© 2006 by Abbie Smith
International Standard Book Number: 1-59052-669-4

Cover design by Kirk DouPonce, DogEaredDesign.com
Interior design and typeset by Katherine Lloyd, The DESK
Unless otherwise indicated, Scripture quotations are from:

The Holy Bible, New International Version © 1973, 1984
by International Bible Society,
used by permission of Zondervan Publishing House

Other Scripture quotations are from:
The Holy Bible, *English Standard Version* (ESV)
© 2001 by Crossway Bibles, a division of Good News Publishers.
Used by permission. All rights reserved.
The Holy Bible, New King James Version (NKJV)
© 1984 by Thomas Nelson, Inc.
The Message by Eugene H. Peterson © 1993, 1994, 1995, 1996, 2000
Used by permission of NavPress Publishing Group
All rights reserved.

Multnomah is a trademark of Multnomah Publishers
and is registered in the U.S. Patent and Trademark Office.
The colophon is a trademark of Multnomah Publishers.
Printed in the United States of America

For information:
MULTNOMAH BOOKS
12265 ORACLE BOULEVARD, SUITE 200
COLORADO SPRINGS, CO 80921

Library of Congress Cataloging-in-Publication Data

mith, Abbie, 1981-
Can you keep your faith in college? / Abbie Smith.
  p. cm.
ISBN 1-59052-669-4
1. College students--Religious life.   I. Title.
BV4531.3.S65 2006
248.8'34--dc22   2005035657

07 08 09 10—10 9 8 7 6 5 4

TABLE OF **CONTENTS**

Countless investments have made this book possible. I am grateful to each.
Thank you to my family, who supports without condition.
To my friends, who encourage without ceasing.
To Northpoint and Emory, who continue to shape me.
To Multnomah, who believed in a girl's dream and is allowing it to unfold.
Most important, to Christ, who loves to an End I'll never fully grasp. May my days find ruin toward nothing less.

THE **JESUS**-COLLEGE QUESTION

Your new life on campus.

Many call it the best years of your life. No parents, no curfew, no authority—basically no rules. College is four years of football games, fraternity parties, late nights leading to hangovers, and maybe some calculus homework (in case the parents ask). Pretty much everything—who you are, who you will be, the "truth"—is up for grabs. And for the first time, you're in charge.

But what many say are the best years, the church often calls the worst. Research says anywhere from 75 to 90 percent of high school seniors who call themselves Christians will abandon their faith by college graduation. That's devastating, but it also makes sense. One invites you to Communion, the other to communal kegs. Jesus says, "I am the Truth," while college says truth is personal and subjective, if anything at all.

I remember a guy in freshman lit saying, "You can't know God until you've had sex." I think what he meant was, "Do you wanna hook up?" but didn't press the issue. Another said Jesus was a father, but then I got confused when a professor said Jesus was gay and partnered with Buddha. Transitioning to university life is overwhelming as is. Add faith to the mix, and it can be pure chaos.

What's unusual about *Can You Keep Your Faith in College?* is that it introduces other students who are walking into that chaos with you. These voices aren't your youth pastor or parent. They're simply students like you, wanting to join in your conversations, assignments, coffee dates and late-night study sessions, where the spoken or unspoken question is: Can Jesus and college go together?

None of the contributors in *Can You Keep Your Faith in College?* pretend to have all the answers, and most still have huge unanswered questions. But at the core of these pages, there's a streamlined realization they don't want you to miss. In short, it's that God is alive and well across every campus of this country.

This book began with a chocolate Easter bunny. The bunny was me.

I was raised in a nonreligious home, and aside from an eating disorder and breaking an ankle in eighth grade, my life was perfect. I had loving parents and a great group of friends, and I seemed to do well in whatever I put my mind to. How could life get better?

Well, it did when I was asked to play tennis at Emory University, the college of my dreams. In simple terms, I left high school as the chocolate bunny you get at Easter. I was perfect, put together, and whole. But I was also hollow.

My journal called it a "void." I didn't even know if I believed in God at the time, but I started asking questions and realizing maybe this life wasn't *it*. Maybe there was something *beyond life* that I was missing? I'd grown up in the South and attended a

Catholic high school, so I'd heard the "Jesus bit," but never quite connected. One fall semester, three words changed that.

1) A crush. Yeah, I fell hard for a guy. I would go where he went and do what he did. But it became quickly apparent that it was Jesus *in the guy* who I'd actually fallen for.

2) Community. I'd been on a lot of teams and in a lot of close relationships, but had never known community quite like the group of Christians I was being drawn toward. Sure, the original crush got me there, but then Jesus started getting through to me. And the love I felt among His followers, for exactly who and where I was, caught me totally off guard.

3) Commitment. What I heard that semester wasn't "churchy." It didn't preach at, condemn, or ritualize me. It was about a relationship. It was about a pursuit of God, on the basis of His pursuit of me. Christ had gone to every extreme to defeat a death I couldn't escape and offer a life I could never attain on my own.

I didn't embark on this faith because it seemed good or sounded right. I did it because I encountered Jesus. As a college student and now a student of Christ, I wanted to hear more from people like me.

But there is no book written *for* and *by* college students about faith. So I started e-mailing all the Christians I knew (about fifteen) and asked some questions. What if we put together a collection of student voices on how to keep your faith during the college years? What could we say that would really help? Oh, and would you be willing to contribute?

At first, writing a book *for* students *by* students seemed ingenious. But then it started to seem presumptuous. How could a bunch of twentysomethings who wondered about life and love and often seemed stuck in messes of our own makings give published advice? *We were still here*—still trying to graduate and figure out this Jesus-college mix. We lacked hindsight and had no retrospective wisdom.

Then again (and this brought us back to the ingenious side), *we're still here*—and that says a lot.

One thing led to the next. We put our thoughts together, and then joined our networks to find a broader pool of contributors. By my senior year, I got a call from a publisher.

That brings us to the book you're holding, *Can You Keep Your Faith in College?* The chapters ahead break into categories of life experience you'd find on any campus—Christian or secular. The entries range in tone and experience, like the people who wrote them. Some are funny, some sad, some more formal, some more bloglike. With permission, all entries have been edited for publication, and names and some other specifics have been changed for various reasons. But these people are real, and their stories are being lived out. (For more stories and resources, be sure to check out www.keepingyourfaith.com.)

For some reason, we've been placed on our campuses. Instead of asking only "why" questions, students you're about to meet think you should also ask "how?" *How, with few rules and all freedom, can we pursue the truth with no regrets and follow a Savior with no reserve?*

Following Christ is more than an option. It's a loaded opportunity we don't want to miss.

Chapter 1

THE **TRANSITION**

*S*eems like there are two kinds of transitioners: One loved high school and is scared to death of college, and the other is sick of high school and ready for something new. Either way, though, it's bound to be lonely, overwhelming, and even scary at times. And either way, the transition will mark a huge change. You won't come out the same person you went in as.

College will hold things you've never imagined. You will hear more "isms" (pluralism, satanism, individualism) than you knew existed and face more addictions (drug, alcohol, porn, eating disorders) than you thought possible.

Something I doubt you'll see, though, is addiction to God. It sounds weird, but I don't think you'll find many students wasted on Christ or hungover from a long night of ministry. I'm not advocating it, whatever *it* might look like. I'm just curious why, on campuses so flooded with beliefs and crazy compulsions, this would be the case.

Maybe the new thing you'll encounter is a choice of faith— a choice to believe that Jesus is who He said He is and to cling to the things He said about you. This transition won't be a cake-walk, but it also won't overwhelm God or catch Him off guard. If He's really God, it can't.

—*abbie*

————————

And my God will meet all your needs according
to his glorious riches in Christ Jesus.
PHILIPPIANS 4:19

IF I **FAKE** A SEIZURE, WILL THEY **LET** ME OFF?

SAN DIEGO STATE

Amanda L.

I don't like decisions. Healthy or unhealthy? Better for me or not better for me? God's will or not God's will? Staying undecided seems safer and more under my control.

I fluctuated between wanting to go to college and not wanting to. Mostly it was wanting to, but then there was the day my parents left me at San Diego State and I bawled in the back of my dad's Buick for an hour (that's the "not wanting to" part).

My friend compared it to a roller coaster, and as I thought about it, that analogy made more and more sense. You pay your money, you want to get on, you know it's going to be a thrill, people tell you how amazing it is…but as your turn approaches, your stomach drops. You have thoughts like, *I could duck out now,* or, *Am I really sure I want to do this?* But you stay in line. You're going to be on the next train, and your heart is now in your throat. You try to make light of it…joke a bit…look around at how unafraid everyone else is and think, *I can do this. People do this all the time.*

So you get in the car. Strap in. And you think, *What in the world am I doing? This is a bad idea.*

You can't just hop off, though, so you tell yourself to calm down. Train starts…*click, click, click*….until you find yourself at a more ridiculous angle than you had anticipated. Sweaty palmed, you hang on for dear life. Now you're desperate. You're thinking, *If I fake a seizure, will they let me off?*

Click, click, click…You swear to God you'll never ride one of these %$#@ things again.

That's where I am right now. I am *click, click, clicking* my way to the top of a very scary, very unfamiliar roller coaster. I have no idea what is going to happen when I plunge over that edge. There are some major differences between the roller coaster and my situation though—the main one being that I can be completely confident in the designer, creator, owner, and operator of this particular ride. Instead of a terrifying "carnie" who hasn't seen a toothbrush in weeks, the operator of all these switches and levers is totally trustworthy, loves me beyond measure, and has promised me that He has my best interests at heart ("For I know the plans I have for you…plans to prosper you and not to harm you, plans to give you hope and a future." Jeremiah 29:11).

I may have no idea where this ride will go, but my God, who designed it, built it, runs it, and strapped me securely into my seat, knows perfectly. Because I trust Him, I have nothing to fear. Because He is good, I know I can trust Him, and because I desire that the purpose of my life be to make His name famous, I will stay on this crazy train.

STRUGGLE TO BE REAL

AUBURN UNIVERSITY

Bethany N.

About the first decision I made at my prestigious university was to check the "biology-concentrated pre-med" box for a major. I arrogantly figured I was up for a challenge. After all, I'd graduated in the top one percent of my high school class.

Not long after the first semester of college began, though, I discovered I hated biology, had no understanding of chemical processes, and could barely pass my tests. The semester was a huge wake-up call for me. Admitting that I would never become a successful doctor, I changed my major. I've changed it again since, but the first change was definitely the most drastic—from pre-med to elementary education.

Sometimes you have to understand what is *not* for you, in order to realize what *is* for you.

Looking back, I think I assumed I was some sort of omniscient human. I was a Christian all through high school, and I was sure God was just as interested in my "success" as I was.

My next big breakthrough: I realized I had picked the wrong prestigious university. I didn't belong in some lofty Christian university. All of my best friends had chosen to attend the big state school, where they spent weekends together, walked to classes in their pajamas, and got involved with sincere Christians who were real about their faith. Meanwhile, I was dressing up for class, spending weekends in the library, and attending church with pretentious Pharisees who seemed to have no depth to their faith at all. I figured I could waste a couple more years being miserable where I was, or I could humbly admit I belonged somewhere less...distinguished. I knew that in order to continue on the path of self-discovery, I would have to do it in a place that would allow for it.

So I transferred. I think my decision to transfer schools was the hardest and maybe the most important decision I have ever made. But I have come alive in this new environment, finding a course of study that I love and finding the few, but authentic, Christians on campus to encounter God with.

My life at college has also unearthed other, smaller discoveries. Having roommates has helped me learn some personal strengths and weaknesses in the context of a home. I have learned invaluable lessons about compromise, compassion, communication, and conflict resolution. Having boyfriends helped me understand my relational flaws. Having free hours during the day led me to stumble upon new hobbies, new interests, new passions. Having responsibilities taught me to keep a budget, keep my space clean, keep a healthy diet and exercise regimen, and keep my bills paid.

Now that my college days are about to end, I'm seeing that the most important discoveries about myself have been directly related to my discovering God...and not only discovering Him, but *encountering* Him. During my first two years at the private university, it was a fight to continue hearing the heartbeat of

God every day. It was a struggle to be real (which for me means admitting I'm weak most of the time) when facing those who seemed to have all the right answers about God. Realizing I *needed* Christ desperately led me to trust in Him more, instead of trusting in myself to make something of me. Making all of the changes, both large and small, took courage that came only from Jesus.

God has revealed Himself to me in textbooks, in the world, in roommates, in a community of believers, in professors, and in life. And now I understand that I don't really know anything about anything! That I need Christ to even breathe! That my desire for more of Jesus grows as I discover the greatness of Him, and discover the insignificance of me. That's why I feel that for me, all the big discoveries have been encounters with God Himself.

THE **HARDER** WAY

DUKE UNIVERSITY

James M.

I had just finished my junior year of high school. All I could think was, *Finally, summer is here. I can sleep in and play golf every day—this is gonna be great!* My father, however, saw things differently. Not more than a week after exams were done, we were on the road visiting colleges. We must have visited more than ten schools within a one-week time span. Every gym started looking the same, and every school's statistics began sounding identical. My frustrations came to an abrupt halt, however, when we made our last stop at what turned out to be the school of my dreams—Duke University.

My senior year passed quickly, while acceptance letters arrived and high school graduation came and went. August came, and I found myself moving into a Duke freshmen dorm. I gladly said good-bye to my parents, thrilled with the thought of finally being on my own.

It didn't take long for classes and the threats of college professors to abruptly put a damper on my excitement. I was managing my time with extreme diligence, not wasting a minute, but it still seemed that I would work all day and get nowhere. Although I was studying late into the nights, my grades were lower than I was used to, and I quickly discovered that college wasn't the breeze high school had been. On top of that, I wasn't making many friends. Three weeks into the semester, the eighteen-year-old who couldn't wait to get out of the house was more homesick than ever.

There I was, the son of a retired army officer and a cadet enrolled in Air Force ROTC, crying tears of frustration and loneliness almost every day. I was (and still am) a very unemotional person, but at that point in my life, I honestly struggled to even walk into the cafeteria without breaking down. I was even more humbled by my inability to not burst into tears while speaking to my father on the phone. I had never been so unhappy in my life. I reached out for God during that time, and He gave me enough strength to persevere, but the depression stayed. By Thanksgiving, I had already applied to a state school back home, where I could join my old friends in the "fun" of college. I promised my parents that I would seriously pray before making my decision, but in all honesty, I had made up my mind.

One of my biggest struggles during this time was the awareness of my parents' disapproval of my transferring. This devastated me. Although my stubbornness and rebellious nature strengthened my resolve, I was crushed to not have their support. I had sought their approval my entire life. One afternoon during this time, I wrote a song with these lyrics:

Why do rebellion and independence have to be so closely linked?
Why does maturing require desertion from the army of family?
I have been raised to be released like an arrow from a bow,
Why does that release snap back on his arm as he lets me go?

CHORUS

It seems there is no choice that will end without some pain,
I can go where my heart leads me, and spit in the face of
   my name.
Or I can march on, a soldier, to the cadence of command,
Only to wonder what might have been if I had lived as my
   own man.
Why can't I see the direction that my hands and feet should go?
Should I follow the path that I see best or follow orders as I
   was told?
Will honor be lost if I disobey, and do as I believe?
Will my choice throw mud on a love that could never again
   be clean?

Finally, the hurt I felt got the best of me, and I confronted my father. He apologized, we made amends, and then we began discussing the pros and cons of my decision. I remember him saying, "Don't take the path of least resistance," but that didn't sit quite right. But then my dad asked me a question I will never forget: "Where in the Bible did God ever tell anyone to take the easier way? It was always the harder way."

I paused and realized he was right, but immediately thought of several reasons why that didn't apply to me. About two seconds later, before I ever spoke, the conviction of the Holy Spirit rushed upon me like the weight of the ocean. I found myself laying facedown on the floor, sobbing with the realization that he was right. God *did* want me to take the harder way, and I was to return to Duke. I was not going to "live as my own man"; I was going to live as God's man. In that moment, I felt a closeness with both my heavenly Father and my earthly father that I will never forget. It was the perfect picture of God calling His people to perseverance, while providing the strength and comfort to achieve it.

Upon returning to Duke, I was still scared. It took only a few hours, however, to completely feel God's peace and reassurance in my life, and only a few days to see the amazing evidence of God's promise. I ended up joining a fraternity and enjoying many new friendships, as well as witnessing opportunities that I never dreamed possible. As for the academics, they were still tough, though I managed to adjust and reprioritize my workload. I was also asked to join the leadership team for the Fellowship of Christian Athletes. The members of that team, as well as the rest of FCA, have turned out to be my closest friends.

My time at Duke has been the most challenging time of my life, but by far the most rewarding. The wisdom and maturity I have gained from the horrors of my freshman year have strengthened my faith in more ways than I can count. I can also see what Paul meant in Romans 8:28 a little more clearly: "And we know that in all things God works for the good of those who love him, who have been called according to his purpose." Though the packages may look different, God remains the Giver of good gifts.

NORMAL—IT'S **SO** OVERRATED

PENN STATE

Annette M.

Transitioning to college was rough for me. On the one hand, there was nothing better than leaving home and finally having full independence. But on the other hand, there was nothing scarier than leaving home and having full independence. I didn't even know how to do my laundry.

I grew up in the church, constantly surrounded by Christians. Youth group felt like my middle name, and I'd been in some element of Sunday school since I could remember. But to be honest with you, I was sick of it. By the time I was a senior, I was more excited about "getting away" than pretty much anything else.

The actual transition was pretty abrupt, but I loved it. Literally, with the farewell wave of my hand, I was on my own. Completely on my own. This was the easy part. The harder part came, however, when I tried to figure out a) who was I? and b) what was mine?

Again, I was the church kid, so I just assumed my identity and purpose were solid. Not so much. I wasn't protected from fear, and I certainly wasn't invulnerable to the daily temptations every college student seems to face. Clubs, sex, drinking, cheating, sex—did I already say that?—pornography, masturbation. You name it and it's here. Not here and hidden, but here, *here*. All of a sudden, it felt like so many things that used to seem awful were lurking at my doorstep. And the worst part was, I *wanted* to let them in.

For the first time since I was seven (still don't understand how kids get the whole Jesus thing, but I was one of 'em), I started questioning the most basic elements of Christianity. Plus, everyone always says God will love you regardless, so maybe this would be my "regardless" time.

I wrestled with God my entire freshman year. I kept my bare-minimum motions as a Christian, but the knocks at my door were a lot more appealing. I knew God and I weren't quite lovey-dovey, but I also knew I had all my life to take that route again. For now, though, I wanted to have sex. I wanted to go to parties, drink, and listen to degrading music with immoral lyrics. I wanted to believe the one-night stand would last. Simply put, I wanted to be like every other college student. I wanted to be "normal."

Thank God (literally) that didn't happen. Through His Word and a few committed people, God started peeling away the layers of my quest to be normal. First Peter 2:9 said it best to me: "You are a chosen person, a royal priesthood, a holy nation, a people belonging to God, that you may declare the praises of him who called you out of darkness into his wonderful light." Wow! Two standouts in this became my benchmark.

First, God tells me *who I am*. I searched for almost a year, and every costume I tried on—as many as I could get my hands on—came up ridiculously short. When I learned/relearned who

I was in Christ, though, I realized no identity of this earth—let alone my campus—was going to satisfy. If I've put my faith in Christ, I've become a chosen one, a royal priesthood, a holy nation, a person *belonging* to God. Uhhh, so much of my first year was about trying to belong to something or someone at my school. If God is really telling the truth, though, I no longer belong to this earth or to anything that wants to satisfy me in it. I belong to God. I belong to a set-apart family of His choosing.

Second, God goes on to tell me *why I'm here*—what my purpose is. And as much as I thought I was sick of being told what to do, I was really just sick of *who* was telling me what to do. I'm to "declare the praises of him" who brought me "out of darkness into his wonderful light." If the light of Jesus really brought me out of darkness, I have every reason in the world (and desire) to talk about Him.

Once my heart got a hold of these big truths, my day-to-day existence literally 180'd. I'm far from perfect, but at least now I can recognize temptation's knock and consciously choose whether or not to open. And as for "normal," I'm pretty happy without it. It's *so* overrated.

GO AHEAD
AND **SHAKE** ME!

CORNELL UNIVERSITY

Seth I.

My first few days at college rocked my self-worth and confidence to the core. I grew up with supportive parents who loved and encouraged me even when I made mistakes. I came from a church full of people who believed what I believed, acted like I acted, and valued what I valued. But when I got to college, I was separated from all that. I thought to be a good, successful person, you had to believe in Jesus and go to church, but most of my fellow students believed in relativity and frankly seemed to be doing just fine. If they didn't need Jesus, did I? I felt like my Religion 101 professor constantly misrepresented Christianity, and even though I tried, I didn't know how to defend it. Everything that gave me worth and meaning was being threatened.

It's like that dream where you find yourself standing in front of class without your clothes on. I felt exposed and defenseless as I woke up to the reality that I was in the minority...and that not every good, responsible, intelligent person believes in Christ. It seemed like everything I held dear was being picked apart and deconstructed at every turn.

During that time I came across this passage in the Bible:

> At that time his voice shook the earth, but now he has promised, "Yet once more I will shake not only the earth but also the heavens." This phrase, "Yet once more," indicates the removal of things that are shaken—that is, things that have been made—in order that the things that cannot be shaken may remain. Therefore let us be grateful for receiving a kingdom that cannot be shaken, and thus let us offer to God acceptable worship, with reverence and awe, for our God is a consuming fire.
> HEBREWS 12:26–29, ESV

So two years ago my prayer became, "Okay, God, bring it on! I know You are in control, You have me in the palm of Your hand, and You have given me a kingdom that cannot be shaken. So go ahead and shake me! Shake everything off that can be shaken so that only what cannot be shaken may remain."

Since then, I am convinced that what could have seriously damaged my faith became a trial that has made my faith stronger. God began stripping away what is merely man-made and cultural about my Christianity and started showing me who Jesus Christ is. He keeps my faith secure even when nothing makes sense. Many things have been shaken off that I thought were essential, but now I have a deep confidence in God that cannot be shaken.

WAIT-LISTED

VANDERBILT UNIVERSITY

Erin T.

M y college decision was far from what I expected. As my
senior year of high school approached, I remember caring
about one application only—the one to the University of Notre
Dame. My entire family had gone there, I lived nearby, and I
loved the school spirit. Everything fit perfectly. There were a mil-
lion and one reasons why I knew this school had practically been
built for me. Application submissions came and went, and by the
end of my senior year, I had received acceptance letters from
every school...except one. Notre Dame had placed me on a waiting list. I was shocked. I questioned whether God played any role
in my college decision and if so, why He would make me sit in
torture for the next three months (before I would, hopefully, be
admitted to Notre Dame). Did He not care about my desires or
my dreams to be in school at Notre Dame?

For the first time in my life, I was forced to sit back and trust
God, waiting patiently for the next letter. Patience hasn't ever
been my best quality. It wasn't until much later that I was reluc-
tantly thankful for what God taught me during this process. The
months passed, and I finally received the much-anticipated letter
from Notre Dame. The opening line read, "We regret to inform

that you will not be a part of this year's freshmen class." I felt let down; I felt this new dread of the unknown seep into my stomach and heart. How had God not realized that this was what was best for me?

Come fall, I was one of the last to leave for school, leaving me plenty of time to think about how I was the only one of my friends to be attending a second-choice school. My loneliness and frustration only made matters worse. Transferring after first semester loomed as a strong possibility. When move-in day finally arrived, however, I was pleasantly surprised. My roommate was so sweet, and my dorm was beautiful. After the first month of school, I was even happily involved in one of the campus ministries. God was daily revealing to me the exact reasons He put me on this campus.

I'm sure Notre Dame would have been a lot of fun and certainly would have provided an enjoyable four years. I see now, however, that going to Notre Dame would have been comfortable. My old friends would have been down the hall, my family would have been a car ride away, and essentially, no overt challenges would have been in my life. From day one at Vanderbilt, I have been faced with new challenges in various arenas of my life—most importantly, my walk with God. Every day, I see more and more clearly God's reasoning in placing me here, a dark campus in so many ways, where He longs for His light to be seen.

CURVEBALL

Emory University

Tyler S.

I have always been very thankful for my family. Even as a child, I consistently thanked God for the family I had and assumed it would always be a stable force in my life. Then two weeks before I left for college, my parents sat my brother and me down. My brother and I were expecting the "with Todd going away to college, we're really gonna have to watch our finances" speech. Instead, we received the biggest curveball of our entire lives. My parents said they were separating.

My dad gave everything the sense of being temporary, but I think we all knew none of this was going to be short lived. On that day, both my brother and I realized that the secure foundation we had grown up with was beginning to deteriorate beneath our feet.

Very shaken by the news, I left immediately and went over to a good friend's house. I tried to hold back the tears, but I failed miserably. The looming separation made those final weeks before leaving for school some of the most awkward and difficult days of my life. On the surface, nothing had necessarily changed around the house, but we all knew the truth behind what was going on.

I was finally able to leave for school and temporarily forget what was going on at home. The biggest challenge for me was to accept all of this as a reality that wasn't going to change. The only thing I could—and can—do to continue my healing is to face the facts head-on. This isn't a nightmare I can wake up from and erase; it's a living part of my reality.

Another huge challenge was learning to accept my mother and father for who they were. Unfortunately, my parents battle the same sins that I do every day. It's hard to come to grips with the fact that your parents have weaknesses and imperfections and come from the same broken human race you do.

During my junior year in college, I finally began seeing a counselor who helped me talk about my feelings and thoughts. While I despised the idea of seeing a counselor, the encouragement of a few close friends to do so was such a blessing. I clearly needed guidance on the healing process and a willing ear to listen.

That same year, another curveball was thrown at me when my father remarried. Not only that, but at the wedding he announced the pregnancy of his new wife. I realize that the restoration and learning process of these events is far from complete, but in an unusual way, these circumstances have brought me closer to God. In short, it was easy for me to remain comfortable when my family was intact, but my need and dependency on God became much more apparent when this comfort was taken away.

I am by no means saying that divorce is good or will always have a positive impact on the people involved. I have struggled horribly with many things and continue to face challenges as they arise, none of which would have been an issue had my parents not gotten a divorce. Thankfully, though, God, through Christ, is supreme over everything and somehow wants me to come to Him with my frustrations and troubles. Because of the relationship He wants me to have with Him, He alone serves as my refuge of strength and unfailing comfort. As St. Augustine wrote, "God is so powerful that he can create good out of evil." In the same way, while the impact of divorce on anyone's life would seem totally negative, through God's awesome power and His incomprehensible love for us, He can use it for good.

Chapter 2

THE **CLASSROOM**

I remember quite a few times (mostly late at night) asking God if He really cared about my grades, or even if my purpose really was to be a student. I guess I thought God's agenda for a Christian in college was to spread the gospel. But then again, I wasn't sure. For me, neither skipping class to share the Good News nor skipping quiet times to share coffee with my textbook ever felt quite right.

Here's what I've decided: It's not either/or; it's both/and. College is a time to enrich your understanding and enhance your worldview. It's also a time to spread your wings of faith. In other words, the secular and sacred aren't mutually exclusive. You can be a serious biology major and seriously love Jesus, or a fanatical Democrat and radical Christian.

God's agenda for college remains a mystery at times, but His agenda for life—"going and making disciples"—always gives me a starting point. Something I missed about this statement for a long time, though, is that *going and making* always coincides with *staying and being made*.

I'll say this and leave you alone to hear from more students: You are clearly at college to learn, but when the eternal purpose of your 8 a.m. class comes into question, it helps to remember that Intro to Psych isn't the goal. It's just the road being used to get you there. God cares about the seemingly marginal aspects of your life because He knows they shape extremely major aspects of you.

—*abbie*

"Love the Lord your God with all your heart and with all your soul and with all your mind."

MATTHEW 22:37

WHAT **IF** THERE WERE NO **GRADES**?

NEW YORK UNIVERSITY

Andrew C.

W hat if school weren't required or learning wasn't graded? Would you *really* study more, sleep more, or review harder? Or what if your role as a boyfriend came with no expectations for Valentine's Day—would you still buy the roses? Or as a son or daughter—would you still call home? In simplest terms, what is motivating you to live the way you do?

Jesus calls obedience a response to faith, while the world calls obedience a response to authority. But our commission as Christians is only possible through faithful dependence on Christ's authority (Matthew 28:19). In other words, our obedience is not about duty today; it's about privilege.

Is being a servant of God too small a thing, when He made you a voice to the "Gentiles" and a light of the world (Isaiah 49:6; Matthew 5:14)—an heir with Jesus and an expression of His life?

Jesus is not asking for good grades today. He's not asking us for religious effort or forced discipline. He's asking for *us*. He's asking you and me to let Him step inside our moments so that He might make much of our days.

The question is, Are we willing to receive *much*?

And the next question is, Are we willing to let go of *us*, in order to make much of *Him*?

So, sending flowers for Valentine's is great, but sending flowers on a random day because you want to is even better. Same goes for calling home and caring about grades. Being motivated by God's love is more powerful than any requirement.

LOOKING FOR ANSWERS

UNIVERSITY OF SOUTHERN CALIFORNIA

Steve P.

For a while after I became a Christian, I was unsure of what my purpose was. I didn't know what I was supposed to do with my life. Some people told me the primary job of a Christian was to make disciples of other people, but that didn't make any sense to me. Why would God create a bunch of people with the main purpose of their lives being to go around trying to convince each other that He exists? Clearly God must have a higher purpose in creating us than that. So why are we here? I read book after book and asked numerous people the same question, and the only answer that made any sense (or seemed biblically based) was that we were created to worship Him.

But what does that mean? Should I hole myself up in a chapel somewhere for the rest of my life and sing worship songs? If we're just supposed to worship Him, why would He create each of us so differently? Why would He create this world so intricately? Why wouldn't He just create a world full of churches and give everybody the ability to play the piano and guitar and sing well? Why would He give us such complex lives and make us such complex people? I was incredibly confused, until I started to understand what worship really meant.

I realized that God created a solar system so large that our earth looks like a tiny speck, and then He created a galaxy so massive that you can't even see our solar system in it, and then He created a universe so infinite that you can't see our galaxy in it; but He also created a very detailed universe. Scientists broke our cells down into atoms, then subatomic particles, then quarks and strings—and they're still going! The point is that God is incredibly creative and infinitesimally concerned. Just look around you—this world is so unnecessarily complex. God could have made us all stick figures, but it's not in His nature to be uncreative. So why do we worship as though we follow an unimaginative God? Why is our worship so one-dimensional? Why do we limit our concept of worship to songs? God meant for every act of ours to be an act of worship. Poetry, art, dance, speaking, writing, working, studying, conversing with friends—we can glorify God through all of these. Anything we do can be an act of worship.

I remember when I was little, my parents would always pray before any big event (a piano recital, a big test, a big game coming up) that I would use it to glorify God, but I never really understood that prayer. What does playing the piano have to do with God? How does God benefit from me scoring a basket? But now I understand: Whatever we do for God is an act of worship to God. God calls us all to be worshipers and to worship Him in the way that will most bring glory to His name. For most people, that probably isn't music. So what are you good at? What do you do daily? Use that to glorify God, not yourself. That's why He made you.

People tell me that being a Christian is too difficult, and if you limit Christianity to a set of laws and boundaries you need to follow, then I understand how someone could actually believe that. But all God really wants us to do is praise Him, and if you look around, you'll see that He's given us a lot of inspiration. So praise Him. Praise Him alone in your room with a guitar, or onstage in front of thousands. Praise him by filling an easel with an explosion of beautiful colors, or by filling a page with amazing poetry. Praise Him when you are at work or studying alone in the library. Praise Him when the sun is raging and the hills look beautiful, or when the rain is pouring down and the grass is green. Praise Him in your e-mails, in your blogs, and with your friends. Let everything that has breath truly praise the Lord! That's worship—that's why you and I were made.

THE **THING** ABOUT MOUNTAINS

University of Georgia

Brett L.

I came to college having no idea what I wanted to do with my life, but figured it would become clear after taking classes or pursuing my interests. I came up negative on both. It's now my third year, and I still have no idea. But then I talked to a thirty-year-old who *still* had no idea, which got me thinking—maybe the point of life isn't figuring out what you want to do with it. Proverbs 16:9 says, "In his heart a man plans his course, but the LORD determines his steps"—so no matter how much my parents, friends, professors, or even I myself nag me about my lack of direction, I can still know God is controlling my steps. (This is comforting for the most part, but also unnerving, because if God controls my steps, I don't. But that's another topic...)

People always say, "Faith can move a mountain," but I was usually the one making fun of them and saying that statement was merely pretty "New Testament talk" with some nature imagery thrown in to entice the granola crowd (myself included). God is starting to show me otherwise. Whenever

I'm struggling to maintain perspective on the "mountains" of life, I always doubt God's power. Does He really care that I'm battling like this or understand how this is affecting/defecting my relationships, with Him included? Because if He did, He wouldn't allow them to keep happening.

God's typical response lately has gone something like this: "No, it's actually your lack of faith that allows the lacking perspective. Actual faith allows you to see, or move, beyond the mountain into My gaze. In other words, when you have faith in Me (i.e., choose to believe the unseen, as I explain in Hebrews 11:1), you see the unseen. You see through the mountain. Beyond the mountain. Between the mountains. A mountain fades into a hill—a doable task…"

Time may be the cure for our perspective problem. But I think faith is better. Faith puts our mountains back into the hands of the mountain Maker.

Back to my original struggle: I still have no idea where life is going to lead me. But I'm becoming more convinced that God will not only mark the steps to follow, but He'll also provide one heck of a view along the way.

JESUS AND PLATE TECTONICS

WASHINGTON UNIVERSITY IN ST. LOUIS

Steven R.

E nvironmental science was a distribution requirement. I hated it. One early Tuesday morning, our teacher was lecturing on the idea that plate tectonics was the cause for everything in existence. Half-asleep, a friend sitting next to me sarcastically joked, "Oh, so Jesus appeared out of the rocks, huh?"

People around him chuckled, and even our professor put on a sort of half grin. He went on, however, to explain that not only earth's creation, but also the creation of interactions, relationships, even emotions on earth, point back to this theory. I wasn't out to bash science, or plate tectonics (well...), but I certainly wasn't about to base my existence on the spontaneous collision of plates, either.

Actually, I'm convinced that science and religion can coexist. Who knows—maybe God ordained the whole plate tectonics thing. Then we could both be happy. Sort of.

My point, though, is the impression my friend made on me when he spoke up in class about his beliefs. He wasn't fazed by the professor's title, or his classmates' laughter. He was fazed by Christ's death. Calling yourself a Christian sets you up for ridicule. It's exclusive and in most ways illogical (like, typically in life, you don't just *get* things when you haven't earned them, especially semi-important things like eternal life).

One of Starbucks marketing mottos says: "We're known for our coffee, but our people make us famous." Change a few words, and I think we could make a church's life motto: "We're known as a house of God, but our people make Him famous."

Speaking up isn't easy (you didn't see me doing it), but it doesn't get us anywhere to be silent. We are witnesses of Jesus Christ. Not could-be witnesses or should-be witnesses—we *are* witnesses (Acts 1:8). You could be a good one, or you could be a bad one, but at the end of the day, you're still a witness. Erwin McManus says, "The greatest threat to the movement of Jesus Christ is Christianity." Jesus will not rise and fall on the doing (or undoing) of a religion, church, or campus ministry. His lordship will not change by way of a theory or movement. God will be God throughout all generations. What can change, however, is the fame of Jesus and our familiarity with His lordship. The question, then, that I'm trying to plaster on my heart is, "When will I stop bowing to the feared idols around me and start rising to the fame of Jesus Christ?"

As college students and major players in the church, we have a mighty task before us: to allow the infinite Christ to preach to our generation by means of His people.

DEEP BREATH

FURMAN UNIVERSITY

Alisha T.

C ollege makes it hard not to live in the "real world." Everything about it points to "the job afterward" or "moving
the résumé forward." I'm not here to bash college as a prepara-
tory tool or its impact on our futures. I am here to bash viewing
these years as the "end all" for our futures. Everyone and their
mom will tell/has told you otherwise, but you don't have to
have a graduate degree to get a job.

We all know rich, happy people, and we all know rich,
unhappy people. Similarly, we all know smart people with good
jobs and smart people with not-so-good jobs. The point is, the
world's definition of health, wealth, and prosperity doesn't
always have a happy ending. As it relates to us, graduating first
in your class, or last in the rankings, doesn't determine your
happiness, either.

Side note: The small Himalayan kingdom of Bhutan has a
new take on all this. They've replaced GDP (Gross Domestic
Product) with GNH (Gross National Happiness) in order to
determine the well-being of their nation (Google "Gross National
Happiness" for more info. Pretty funny).

Anyway, if "success" on paper doesn't determine happiness

and security for our futures, why should we waste our time with college at all? If God's gonna do what God's gonna do, why should I waste time suffering in the library?

Bottom line—I think God cares about where you *are*, more so than where you're going. If you're in college, I think He's saying: "Go after it! Make the best of it! Try your hardest and trust Me with the results. Take your daily bread and quit waiting for the Last Supper. Your future will be a feast, I promise."

Imagine you died tomorrow. I doubt anyone at your funeral would mention your good grades, solid list of contacts, or highest honors in your major. Rather, I think people would talk about who you were as a person, how you interacted as a human being—with honesty, purity, spiritual sensitivity, wisdom, patience. We waste so much time on fading obsessions (read the book of Ecclesiastes), when there's a world of true life and infinite possession.

I say, lay down your GPA and stop trying to market your future. Six figures aren't all they're cracked up to be, and finishing first isn't always the best end. Don't hear me say we should stop studying or start skipping class, but we need to take a deep breath.

God is good. He believes in you. And He cares about the precise details of your future.

LESSONS
IN BOOT CAMP

GORDON COLLEGE

Ann C.

M y alarm clock sounded a shrill battle cry. Tense and alert, I sat straight up in bed, clutching my graphite weaponry. I looked down and saw crumpled loose-leaf pages, along with sharpened pencils, which had left smudge marks on my sheets overnight. I rubbed my dry eyes and crawled out of bed. All around me were opened books, unfinished paragraphs, and website references. I, a new cadet involuntarily conscripted into the army of literature, was suffering some serious battle wounds.

Let me start from the beginning. I walked into my freshman poetry seminar on a regular Thursday afternoon ready to begin my academic boot camp. I had my necessary reserves. I had even brought notes from my high school advanced placement English classes to give me the edge on my fellow soldiers of education. I was armed; I was ready; I was fired up and prepared to jump the hurdles of grammar, climb the ropes of creative thinking, and target the concept of active reading. Poetry was my passion, the one subject in school worth fighting for. I would fall on my sword for a sonnet by John Keats, and I was certain my valiant efforts would produce medals of honor.

Well, there comes a day when every good soldier is sent to the front, and my call came on Thursday. Our poetry professor assigned us our first paper, and like any other giddy new recruit, I was anxious to make him proud. For the next few days, I stayed in my dorm room in solitary confinement, eyes glued to my computer, reciting poems and looking up data in an attempt to compare modern poetry with styles of the past. Writing essays about comparing works of literature was my strongest skill! I poured my soul into that paper. When I handed my superior those precious four pages, I was sure he would be just as proud of my work as I was.

The next time we had our call to order, my professor explained that he wanted to conference with us individually about our papers. His voice sounded resigned and negative, but I assumed he was talking to the rest of class. Surely he couldn't be referring to my masterpiece! I smiled to myself. I knew that paper was a tank, and nothing could touch it.

As it turns out, the paper was not a tank. The truth is, it wasn't even a bow and arrow. My English professor tore that essay apart like he was a foreign spy with highly classified information. As I walked out of his office after our conference, I felt the tears fall like nuclear bombs. Okay, a good fighter never cries, but I couldn't hold back my disappointment. A huge part of my soul was in that paper. I had failed as a cadet, and I began to question whether I even belonged in college. Could I handle it? Would I ever have what it takes to succeed?

This brings us to the next morning, when I woke up groggy and in a whirlwind of emotions. My confidence had been shattered, and I was faced with a huge decision. I was either going to continue my training or quit and go home.

But that morning I made some breakthroughs. I realized, for example, that I had been approaching my school assignments for myself, desiring to highlight my own talents, seeking to earn affirmation and praise for *me*. What would it be like if my goal in every homework assignment was to glorify God? If I could fully understand my worth in Christ's eyes, rather than in the eyes of the university faculty, my parents, or even my peers? What if I had been able to receive that constructive criticism with joy, realizing that the conference with my teacher was a gift from God?

I am slowly learning to allow God to ready me for battle, desiring that my efforts be pleasing to Him alone. Although college can seem huge, overwhelming, and stressful at times, I remember where my strength comes from. So, "finally, be strong in the Lord and in his mighty power.... Put on the full armor of God, so that when the day of evil comes, you may be able to stand your ground, and after you have done everything, to stand" (Ephesians 6:10, 13).

YOU **AND** ME

SEATTLE PACIFIC UNIVERSITY

Yih L.

I'm looking for my son, my daughter,
someone to love like no other, someone to call my
captivating, my darling, my beautiful, my self.
I'm looking for myself through the weeds that leave
my home-born dandelions worn, torn up against the thorns,
just looking for a place to
breathe in
and breathe out
the oxygen that is me, the oxygen that is my life,
and the only response left for you is to
hyperventilate because you cannot get enough of me,
you cannot even demonstrate or calculate your need for me
but in gasps of air, struggling to live without me,
but hold up, slow down, wait up, calm down,
as I allow this cadence in our love fest between lover and beloved
past the good times and the bad times ahead,
I ask of you, How much of me will you devour?
How much of me will you allow to carry you this hour?
Bring me your flowers in the form of kisses,
so that I may be wrapped up in your lips

as you envelop my soul with your tongue of truth, dripping,
    diving,
seeping, soaking my wounds from my father
and my mother and my church
as your saliva searches through the nooks and crannies of my
    inner being,
past the "What's your name?" and
"Where are you from?" and
"What's your major?"
when my heart is screaming out for some major help
in the form of a hug, in the form of something,
anything to show me that you care.
I am laid bare, wrapped in the fetal position of despair.
Will you be more than hollow promises of affection
simply reflecting the choruses of Jessica and Ashley Simpson?
Will you kick me to the curb and leave me by the wayside?
or will I somehow find that you and I collide?
So I reply by asking you, How long have you been chasing me
    breathtakingly?
How exactly wonderful do you wish this hour alone with me
    will be?
The wonder of life with me is
life, electrical shocks run through your veins and arteries
unlocking the imagery of a spiritual process of photosynthesis
because like I said, I am your oxygen,
you can't even begin to rap cuz I've got you so wrapped up in
    me in you in me in you.
You start spitting rhymes like "Ch-ch m-m-m-mike 1 2?"
Can you feel my caress to compress my infinite love for you
in these similes and these metaphors you can understand?

Digest them in, express them back, profess them up
to the heavens as they are interwoven with Beethoven-like
  symphonies,
and I will stretch my hand out back toward you from eternity,
and in the process, waking up the protozoa of hope and faith,
exploding into a supernova of love and grace.
And you still wonder how this hour alone with me will be?
Birds soar into my majesty and fish dive into my regal blue seas,
grass dances to my violins of the wind
and crickets jam to the voices that I've placed within.
And it is the jealousy within me that not only
wants to make this hour fabulously marvelous,
but I will travail to set you free and prevail in uniting
you with the Christ, uniting you with me.
And here is all of me for all of you,
but only you can delay, only you can obstruct, only you can
  hinder.
How fully can you not be afraid and surrender?
Fill my mind with your mind to the last crevice
so that it may create a new genesis
and develop an antithesis to me and my story.
Catch me into your arms so that I may let go and float
into your sea of sweet cantaloupe
that my taste buds begin to rejoice in the hope that is
succulent in my times of turbulence,
and it is in these times that I find none that is
equivalent to you, my nerves
are exploding in cataclysmic proportions.
I will not allow my life to be another spiritual abortion,
so I cling to your power to make this hour

terribly glorious because
I'm sick of being notorious for being a man all about me
so make me victorious over the man that is me.
Allow me to attempt to hold you
to the point where I'm tempted to no longer hold you,
so I fall into you and I am at rest
when I am you and you are me.
Swathe me into your heart, restart my
mind in a level unknown that is beyond infinity,
that is you, that makes e=mc^2 like 2 + 2 compared to you.
Allow me and you to begin our dramatic comedic romantic
    adventure-like fusion
as your heart begins the percussion of the drumbeats of my
    heartbeats
and it continues to beat
and it continues to beat
and it continues to beat
and it continues to beat
to the revelations of your ongoing passions
that is you
that is me
this is me in you
this is you in me
and that is why I sing!

MISSED **ASSIGNMENT**

LOYOLA COLLEGE

Laura F.

I am very driven. My constant temptation is to bury myself in homework in order to fulfill my academic expectations.

One evening, one of my hall mates and I were talking, and she explained how much she longed for the love of a man, having never experienced that love from her father. I dumbly listened and missed the perfect opportunity to tell her of the love of God. That night, realizing the opportunity I had missed, I cried myself to sleep as I prayed that God would give me another chance to tell this precious girl about God's perfect and all-sufficient love for her.

The next night I went to church, despite having a ten-page paper due the next morning that I had yet to start. I couldn't escape the conviction that God wanted me to go. After the sermon, a random student got up and explained that he thought God just wanted the congregation to be reminded of His love. He explained God's love in such a profound way that my heart and mind were literally giddy for the rest of the night—so much so that upon arriving home, my roommate couldn't help but ask what had happened at church. I was able to explain to her that God had freshly reminded me about His love.

That was one of the first times I'd tangibly realized the joy derived from obedience. God also used it to remind me that regardless of where I am or how fruitless I seem to be, He is endlessly watching over my life. Exhausted and with no paper in hand, I went to sleep, entrusting my paper to God.

I kid you not—I woke the next morning having dreamt the plans for the paper. I had a lot of writing assignments that semester, but this one was by far the best.

Chapter 3

THE **DORM**

I vividly remember my first college shower. I'd been to summer camp and grown up with a mom and a sister, so living with girls wasn't the issue. I stepped out of my room with a pink, fuzzy layer of protection and containers of shampoo and conditioner and soap in hand. Two steps behind me came another toweled specimen, yet this one was in hunter green. *He* proceeded to ask me about my day, and then asked about my weekend plans.

Was this a joke? Conversations with guys made me skeptical enough (I'd been forewarned about my "fresh-meat" status), but on the way to my morning shower? Bathing rituals have yet to return to their original status.

Like it or not, living in community exposes you. Literally. In so many ways, it's one of the most challenging experiences you can have. Parts of it are like a perpetual slumber party, and other parts are exhausting, depressing, and downright annoying. I had a roommate who was drunk more often than she was sober— that was annoying—but it also became the most authentic and life-changing relationship I've ever had.

You can't hide when you're having a bad day or simply escape when you're in a crappy mood. You can't say one thing Sunday and get away with another the rest of the week. There are no closed doors and no fig leaves to duck behind. When you live in community, you are onstage around the clock.

At the end of the day, we're all witnesses to something. It can be a good something or a bad something, but regardless, your witness is there. What's yours?

—abbie

The LORD will fulfill his purpose for me;
your love, O LORD, endures forever—
do not abandon the works of your hands.

PSALM 138:8

EMBARRASSED
BY JESUS

UNIVERSITY OF COLORADO

Dana W.

I t's always fun to introduce "different-circled" friends, so while
out to dinner recently, I indulged in such an opportunity. Jill
is Jewish and engaged in her faith from a cultural standpoint, but
remains spiritually detached. Nathan, on the other hand, fits the
phrase "Jesus freak" better than I fit my name. A lot of times I
love this about him, but many times (this being one), I hate it.
His overt, borderline obnoxious "evangelizing" has left me hugely
embarrassed on more than one occasion.

Before the first fork took rise, Nathan launched the bomb.
"So, Jill, what do you think about God?"

Turning beet red, I frantically tried to drum up a diversion.
Maybe I could spill a drink across the table. Wouldn't work...who
created waiters and sponges, anyway? My second thought was
climbing under the table to cry. Okay, that didn't happen, either.

Bottom line—I was embarrassed. Nathan had been intru-
sive to Jill's belief system.

Eventually, I found space to squeeze in an interruption and
led the remainder of the dinner conversation in a direction
devoid of any proselytizing or God-ish discussion.

As we left the restaurant and Nathan went his separate way, I let out a huge sigh of relief and apologized to Jill. "Honestly, I had no idea he was going to do that."

"Do what? I thought he was great."

"You thought the food was great?" I asked.

"No, I thought Nathan was great."

"You did?"

"Yeah—do you mean because he brought up religion?"

"Well, yeah. He completely invaded your beliefs!" I couldn't believe what I was hearing.

But she set me straight. "Honestly, even though I don't agree with everything Nathan said, the fact that a college student has such strong notions about *anything* was amazing to me. Sounds crazy, but I'm tempted to say I think that's what makes me respect a person! Nathan asked what I believe, which made me feel cared about, as well as challenging me on something I'm not even sure about. Don't take this the wrong way, but I was even upset when you changed the conversation. I felt like we were just getting started!"

Wow! I'm not sure I've ever felt like such a coward.

Jill basically described the very thing she enjoyed about Nathan as that which I was ashamed of. She was drawn to his conviction about his faith. He stood for something and was enthusiastically living it.

Nathan may never win the Most Eloquent Conversationalist Award or take the stage at a Billy Graham crusade, but his "freakish" faith speaks volumes compared to the silence of mine. He understands our gospel in such a way that he'll make any attempt—foolish, even—to proclaim his Savior.

I long to be a freak again.

JESUS AND
TAKE-OUT CHINESE

WHEATON COLLEGE

Erica S.

God gave me three great roommates this year. I prayed all summer about learning to share my faith and doing so clearly. I knew my relationship with God had gotten stronger, and I wanted to make sure they saw the difference. I won't bore you with the details, but I learned two very important lessons about this early on (both through painful experiences).

First, I don't need to set up God-talks. They happen if my "walk" is happening. Even on my most organized day, I could've never predicted, or planned for, the impromptu conversations thrown at me this year. Why do I get up early to read the Bible? Why don't I drink? Do I ever get mad at people? How can I be so confident in something I can't prove?...and so many more, at so many random points of the year. Wow—fun questions, but also completely overwhelming! My current prayers are for wisdom to know answers, instead of wondering whether or not someone will ask. "I could never see, hear, or conceive of what God has prepared for we who love him" (1 Corinthians 2:9, personalized). Knowing, then, that He has some cool things in mind, I want to "always be prepared with an answer for the reasons I call myself a Christian" (1 Peter 3:15, paraphrased).

My second big wake-up call was realizing steady passion leads to influence. When people see other people living alternative lives, it's intriguing. And if they see them doing so over a consistent period of time with a consistent level of passion, they can't help but take interest. Walking the walk you talk makes people follow.

I'll end with this story. It was a late Sunday night over take-out Chinese. My roommate laid it out that she knew something was different about me. Unable to put a finger on it, she wanted me to explain what this was all about. She figured it was about the "Jesus thing," but if that was true, she could never "do it." She could never be *that* good or become *that* religious. We spent most of the night discussing that it would never be about how good she could be or how much she could do, but it was about how perfect Jesus was and how much He had already done. My roommate accepted Christ as her Lord and Savior that night. I kid you not—the next week we started reading the Gospel of John, and two weeks later, a Bible study started on our hall.

This may be coming off too by-the-book Christian-y, but I promise it's true. I could've never planned this and certainly didn't do anything special to see it unfold. The formula was as simple as me being drawn to a Savior (or maybe just good Chinese food) and her being drawn to passion. That's it.

"He who began a good work in you will carry it on to completion until the day of Christ Jesus"
PHILIPPIANS 1:6.

Believe that today.

RISKY BUSINESS

ARIZONA STATE

Brandon M.

There is a fairly popular Christian radio station in L.A. (although it comes through in most major cities) whose tagline is, "Safe for the whole family." This describes, in my opinion, the greatest reason for our failure to connect with non-Christians, especially in a college setting. There is nothing in the Bible that even implies that God is "safe." Jesus never claimed to offer safety, comfort, or prosperity in exchange for following Him. In fact, following Him seems like the riskiest thing we can do. For ten of the eleven disciples who were with Him to the end, that meant dying for their faith. For John the Baptist, it meant being beheaded. For Paul, it meant being severely flogged and beaten many times, then dying in prison.

I wouldn't call that "safe for the whole family."

After dedicating my life to God my freshman year, I faced a dilemma. It's one I feel most Christians in college struggle with—how should my faith affect my relationship with non-Christians? I figured the best thing to do would be to imitate what the Christians around me were doing, so I hung out almost exclusively with Christians. I started talking in Christianese phrases. I felt like all my conversations had to be deep or spiritually based, and I tried to act like I was flawless and perfect. Well, that didn't work.

After a while of failing, I realized I had conformed myself to Christians instead of to Christ. Christ hung out largely with tax collectors and prostitutes. He didn't tie Himself in any way to the main religion of His time, and He acknowledged the brokenness of all mankind.

This realization brought me a lot of freedom and radically changed the way I relate to non-Christians. Subsequently, I've had many conversations with people who hate Christianity, or who fell away from Christianity. Typically, I find that their problems are with Christians, *not* with Christ. The more amazing thing to me, though, is that what turns them off *should* turn them off. They're reacting to attitudes and behaviors that are directly contradictory to the nature of Christ: "Christians don't really care about people," "They don't care about the poor," "I feel like Christianity is just a list of 'dos' and 'don'ts,'" "They are hypocritical," "They are judgmental," and on and on.

When I hear other people talk about my faith like that, it sounds just like the sort of dead religion that Christ came to this earth to abolish in the first place.

I think one of the great tendencies when we are trying to live as a Christian in a non-Christian environment is to detach ourselves from the world and try to fit in with the other Christians. But living as Christ did often means the opposite—sticking out from both the religious and the nonreligious in your community. That's serving a God who is anything but safe.

A PRETTY
RIDICULOUS IDEA

GEORGE FOX UNIVERSITY

Dan B.

I excitedly told God when I had finished sorting out my schedule, "See that hour right in the middle of the day—that's all yours!" And it actually was...for about a week. But inevitably, the meetings, lectures, and various other options gradually started popping up, and the old "quiet time" was pushed off until later. I began using that midday hour to catch up on schoolwork, assuring God I'd sit down with Him at night, or when stuff became less hectic.

Well, of course things never got less hectic, and the nights always seemed to bring more distractions, like late-night conversations with the girl down the hall or video games with the guys. Point being, my quiet times were consistently neglected. After finally being convicted, or at least finally becoming aware of the conviction, I knew I needed to get back on track.

Some suggested spending time with God before bed. My busiest hours were 10 to 2 a.m., though, so that was out. Between pretty girls, noise, and just plain distraction, *silence* seemed impossible *to hear*. A guy discipling me suggested I get up before class to be with God. The idea seemed ridiculous, but I also knew something pretty ridiculous had to be done. Psalm 5:3 says, "In the morning, O LORD, you hear my voice; in the morning I lay my requests before you and wait in expectation." Mark 1:35 reads, "Very early in the morning, while it was still dark, Jesus got up, left the house and went off to a solitary place, where he prayed."

Seemed to be a trend.

My decision came down to a simple choice: Which was more important—sleep or God? I knew that if I gave Him one hour of my daily twenty-four, He'd do something cool with it. I was right and can honestly say two things: 1) I usually wake before my alarm now anyway, and 2) what was once a discipline is now a desire. Seriously.

MY YEAR WITH A GAY ROOMMATE

PENN STATE

Damien R.

D uring my third year, Gary was my roommate, and Gary was gay. Not "closet" gay or "let's build our friendship and I'll tell you my secret later" gay, but a proud, flamboyant, homosexual male. Gary adamantly claimed his identity in one of our first conversations.

Granted, I've always felt like I was pretty open-minded and certainly open-hearted in my stance as a "hate the sin, love the sinner" Christian. But this one threw me for a loop. I'd heard a lot of opinions on gays and had a lot of opinions about gays and the church, but I'd *never* heard this opinion or had this conversation with the gay person himself—and certainly not the one I was *living* with.

Gary and I got along from day one. I tried to respect his ways of living, and likewise, he was always courteous about mine. We laid our convictions on the table pretty early, just to avoid the major, midyear surprises. I must say one of the funniest, or should I say most awkward, nights of the year was Valentine's Day. I invited a girl over for dinner, and he invited a guy over to watch a movie. As it turned out, we all had a really great time together.

Gary actually enjoyed the fact that I was a Christian and even began asking some core questions about the gospel and the life of Christ. He had been raised in an agnostic home and only had the knowledge of Christians as the "anti-gay" group. The more I hung around with his friends, and similarly, the more I talked with my Christian friends, the more I realized how true this sentiment really was.

It might offend you, but I think Christians can be the most un-unified and judgmental people on the planet. But these are two qualities that grossly oppose the life and teaching of Jesus. Being gay may be difficult to understand, but nonetheless, in the eyes of God, homosexual choices are a sin…like my being a jealous and prideful person is a sin. But does my church and body of fellowship turn me away because I'm a sinner? No! This is the very reason that I need fellowship and community, and the very reason that Christ died in the first place! As He tells us in Luke 5:31, "It is not the healthy who need a doctor, but the sick," and in Romans 3:23, "For all have sinned and fall short of the glory of God." The body of believers exists for support, encouragement, accountability, and prayer; it seeks God's freedom over sinful areas of our lives.

There are a lot of people who struggle with homosexual or bisexual tendencies. As I learned more about the roots and difficulties of the gay lifestyle, God led me to some guys in my ministry who were struggling with this very sin. It's not an easy issue to confront. And it's certainly not one that we as Christians often mention. But as I continue to see the power of prayer and intervention in the lives of these individuals, I become more convinced of God's desire for us to love and pray for them, as creations of His hand.

Turned out, Gary was one of the biggest blessings of my dorm experience. I pray for him a lot and really believe deliverance is coming. Like any lie that grabs hold of us, knowing what's really *true* (about ourselves and everything else) is a long journey and one we'll fight forever on earth. But fixing our gaze on the infinite power and truth of the cross ensures our victory. "Who shall separate us from the love of Christ? Shall trouble or hardship or persecution or famine or nakedness or danger or sword?... No, in all these things we are more than conquerors through him who loved us" (Romans 8:35, 37).

PARTY GIRLS

WASHINGTON STATE UNIVERSITY

Jessica W.

I thought I was tolerant of the girls on my hall. I knew they drank, smoked, and did things with guys I hadn't even conceived of, but I remained civil to them and just avoided their company as much as possible. They would do their thing on weekend nights, and I would do mine. One fall day, however, about halfway through the semester, I came to see this avoidance in a painfully new light.

It seemed like a typical Sunday morning, where no one would wake till noon, making my church preparations a somewhat peaceful and certainly quiet experience. That morning, however, I was surprised to hear the hall door open abruptly, followed by the loud voices of three girls. They stumbled into the bathroom, stinking of alcohol and cigarettes, wearing outfits that looked more like small strips of material than actual clothing. Two of the girls headed straight for the toilet. One glanced at me briefly, but all three were obviously embarrassed to see me. The third girl headed to the farthest sink, avoiding any eye or vocal contact.

I finally spoke up and asked if everything was okay.

After an empty glare, the girl at the sink calmly responded,

"Are you kidding? You're actually interested in how we're doing? You've noticed something other than your church activities or perfect little life? In fact"—she continued, her voice becoming increasingly sarcastic but equally serious—"I can't even believe you're talking to the 'bad girls,' knowing you're so good and would never want to be associated with us."

It hit me like a ton of bricks. My thoughts were immediately taken to numerous stories of Christ and remembering it was the most wretched people who were drawn to Him, the most cast-out who fled to His feet. Where had I gone astray and run so far from the gospel? When did I conclude that I was above the girls in my dorm? How, as a Christian, had I lost sight of imitating Christ?

I slowly walked out of the bathroom that morning, sad and confused about what had happened. Christ died for the sins of the *world*—not only for we who are trying to be sinless, we who act as if we're above and beyond the homeless, the prostitutes, the drug addicts, and the drunkards.

I realized that morning that Jesus' death related more to those girls in the bathroom than it ever had to me. He came that they might have life. He came that they might know grace. All I'd given them was good living and judging looks.

My knees hit that ratty carpet like never before. Tears streamed down my face as I was overcome by new understandings of grace—for me, but maybe more so for them.

Rebuilding trust takes a long time. I can't say the three girls run to me when trouble strikes, but at least they know the door is standing open.

SOLITUDE

David S.

I always find it ironic that high school seniors' greatest fear about starting college is that they'll struggle to find friends. The reality is, you almost can't get away from friends, or at least acquaintances. They may not be of the quality you want, but in terms of finding someone who will connect with something in your life, college is your best bet. Especially in a paid-for, planned-for environment (dorm, fraternity, etc.), community is *expected*. You automatically have "friends."

But I don't think this is necessarily healthy. What's harder, and maybe just as important, is finding time to be alone. When you're in a perpetual community, you can start to mistake all that company for intimacy.

When was the last time you spent an extended period alone? Not *alone* like in the bathroom or driving home for break, but *alone* as in purposeful solitude? When was the last time you took an intentional Sabbath?

Why is this so hard? I think we're afraid of what we might discover about ourselves. But I know that to make the most of college, we need to grow in many ways, including in self-awareness. Some things just don't happen in a crowd.

AMAZING TO THINK

FURMAN UNIVERSITY

Amy L.

I 've been reading the book of Acts lately. What did the early church look like? What happened in those early days of our church that drew *thousands* of people at one time to faith in Christ? What was it that Peter and John and Paul had that was so irresistible that people said, "Yes!" right then and there?

It wasn't a lot of things that might come to mind—looks, clothes, charm, money, or whatever.

Acts 4:13 says, "When they saw the courage of Peter and John and realized that they were unschooled, ordinary men, they were astonished and they took note that these men *had been with Jesus.*" Their lives and characters and abilities were so completely transformed by being with Jesus that they astonished those around them.

Amazing to think that being with Jesus could change me like that...

I read this and wonder, *What stands out about my character that demonstrates that I have been with Jesus? What is radical and different about who I am that will draw people to God? How can I speak so boldly and sincerely that the irresistibility of the truth of Jesus will shine through and overshadow me?*

I want to be transformed by my relationship with Jesus. I don't want it to be just a fact about me—I want it to be the most *obvious* thing about me.

Chapter 4

THE **PRESSURES**

You're *supposed* to rebel in college. Right? And when something is expected, it's that much more justifiable, making it harder to choose something else (even if you know that "something else" would be right). In fact, coming up with an airtight case for your new rebellion is going to be the easiest thing in the world. Trust me.

Doing what you're *supposed* to be doing in college is my definition of peer pressure.

Add to the pressures a lot of untruths, a lot of general murkiness. Life on campus is just so ripe with deceit. In every partial truth (like, "Now's the time to rebel..."), you're likely to find a hidden lie ("...because what you used to believe can't possibly be true").

When it comes to peer pressure—about what you should think and do about success, body image, happiness, relationships, parties, sex, God, you name it—murkiness lies all around.

How do you know what's right, and believe it enough to live it under pressure?

In this chapter you're going to meet students who talk honestly about their struggles to make independent, healthy, godly choices under a lot of pressure to do something completely different. Each of us deals with pressure in different ways and at different points in our character development or circumstances. But we're all on a journey. We can all help each other see through the murk, make it through the pressures. And we have the Light of the world to guide us.

—abbie

Do not conform any longer to the patterns of this world,
but be transformed by the renewing of your mind.
Then you will be able test and approve what God's will is—
his good, pleasing and perfect will.

ROMANS 12:2

BRINK OF EMPTY

UNIVERSITY OF ARIZONA

Leslie R.

We've all got habits. We've all got issues. But I've been carrying around this darn thing as if it owned me (and "darn" is definitely censored). I've tried and I'm tired. I've run and I'm empty. Rock-bottom empty, with no one else to go to and nowhere else to turn. I've dissected the aftermath and analyzed the before-math—to no avail. The demon arises when I arise.

Have you ever felt so trapped that you couldn't get out? So beat down that you couldn't get up? Here I stand. Here I crawl, rather. I find myself in a place of deep shame today, deeply distrusting myself and afraid to trust anyone else. Sin has waged its war against me and apparently won. Christian logic tells me to repent and seek God. Actual logic tells me to screw faith and find a pint of something. Why should I pray, when it's already been done? Why should I seek God, when I've already been beat?

Deep sigh...Good Christian intro. Now I've got us hooked for the "I messed up, but God and I made up" point, right?

No. I'm still in the intro. I'm still in the midnight hour. I've been stripped of every pretense and past-tense and have no point to unveil, or any take-away to offer. And let me say upfront—

I'm not a "flip and find" kind of Bible reader. But lately, random flips have been about all I find the strength to do.

This morning's flip dealt the following find—the following conversation with a voice who cares:

"God, I have no power to face this vast army that is attacking me. I do not know what to do, but my eyes are upon You."…"Do not be afraid or discouraged, my child, because of this vast army, this terrible stronghold. For the battle is not yours, but Mine—march against them. You do not have to carry it. You do not have to cure it. Take up your position, chosen one. Stand firm and see the deliverance I long to give you. Do not be afraid. Do not be discouraged. Go out and face it, for I will be with you. Have faith in Me and you will be upheld. Have faith in My prophets and you will be successful. Trust Me. Believe Me. And in the end, you will recognizably see Me" (2 Chronicles 20:12–17, my paraphrase).

Should we seek God when we're full? Absolutely. But our most intimate moments arrive at the brink of empty, at the brink of being done with ourselves and desperate for God. Prayers at this point can at least lead us toward fullness…not full from my saving, but from my immeasurably full Savior.

I am empty. Fill me, Father.

THE **SECRET**

CLEMSON UNIVERSITY

Tara B.

B ulimia was so easy for me to hide. I grew up in a loving, Christian home and had a positive high school experience. I can honestly say that until college crept up, I didn't struggle with my weight or body image. The college transition was a big one, though, offering various new freedoms and focuses, including those that are food related. For me, this new freedom was accompanied by fear. The topic of conversation at the end of high school and start of college seemed perpetually focused on the dreaded "freshman fifteen."

If you've ever lived on a college campus, it's relatively easy to see how uncontrolled eating can lead to weight gain (as uncontrolled anything can have negative consequences). The dining hall is often a popular social arena, providing a place of comfort and security, and also, unlimited food—not to mention the truthful rumors about late night pizza/study sessions, often accompanied by the latest package of homemade brownies. Finally, the effects of an unknown environment, plus constant conversations about weight, food, and dieting, brought to the forefront of my life an undeniable obsession.

Though the idea would have seemed absurd in the past,

after an unsettling binge one night, I found my feelings of guilt so strong that I went to the bathroom and threw up. Feeling very shameful afterward, I vowed that I would not let this happen again. Two nights later, however, I was up late studying, stressed about a presentation the following day, and sought comfort in my food shelf. There I was, two months into my freshman year, struggling with bulimia, which had quickly become a serious stronghold in my life.

By Thanksgiving break, I was throwing up at least once a day. I knew what I was doing was completely sinful, plus horrible for my body, but the relief of purging had become addicting, and the control factor had blinded my convictions. Essentially, I had replaced seeking God as my comfort in struggles with seeking food. Purging afterward somehow rationalized the shame and disgust I felt over whatever I had eaten. I remained very involved with our campus ministry and even enjoyed meeting weekly with a small group. At this point my bulimia was easy to hide, and I was comforted in knowing I wasn't hurting anyone else.

Already tired of second semester classes and ready for summer weather, spring break brought a much-needed trip home. It included my usual visit to the dentist, but this time it didn't turn out to be so usual. After almost seven months of using bulimia as a scapegoat for my struggles, my throat (and as it turned out, my gastrointestinal track as well) provided an obvious sign to my dentist, and then to my parents, of my hidden disease.

I immediately began meeting with a Christian counselor who had actually dealt with and successfully recovered from an eating disorder herself. My binging and purging bouts slowly decreased, but the hardest thing was the renewal of my skewed mindset and underlying control issues. Strongholds are basically any form of deceit, whether it be something or someone, that distracts from our living relationship with Christ. And deceit is no doubt one of Satan's greatest tools. For me, this deceit was manifested in a stronghold with food that became my means of maintaining control, reaching into virtually every area of my life.

Whether it's a food-related stronghold or anything else, the sole means of killing lies is exposing them. Practical steps may vary, but in the end, freedom can only come when we're willing to loose the chains and *believe* we're really standing as loved and forgiven. Your secret will be found out eventually, so why not expose it now and know you're still loved, forgiven, and justified in the eyes of God, instead of drowning in humiliation in days to come? You don't have to hide anymore. Come into the light.

If you're the one reading this and knowing it's written to you, please hang in there. I know it seems like it'll never end, and it seems like you could never do it. But you can. *You* can't actually, but if you'll be willing to surrender to the One inside you, it will happen. God wants you to be healed more than you'll ever know. He's not overwhelmed by your needs, and He's not surprised by what's going on. Turn toward Him, and from absolute personal experience, I promise He'll turn toward you.

SWEEPING **FLOORS**

University of Rhode Island

Kevin B.

Some of my own issues really, really, really smacked me in the face this week. Like, I find my value completely in what others think of me.

When I realized this junk, I knew in my head that my value lies in Christ. My value is in the fact that I am a loved, beloved, treasured child of God, and if God wants me to sweep floors for the rest of my life in service to Him, it is enough.

BUT I DON'T WANNA SWEEP FLOORS!!!

I want to be bigger, more important, more well-thought-of.

My ego is driving it. My pride is giving it fuel. I am embarrassed—I always want to be the first this and the best that...

Lord, I pray that You will purge this ego pride thing that really reared itself powerfully this week. I want to be satisfied, content, and joyful in sweeping the floors, if that's what You have for me. I don't want to fight against my place if I'm in the place You want me to be in. But I'm not content in it, Lord, and that is sin. My pride and ego have these desires and needs, to be important and valued and all this crap.

Sometimes I listen to worship music and cry, and I'm not sure why. And sometimes I think about You, and the only thing I can say is, "Thank You," and I don't know why.

But, Lord, I'm not consistently turning to You, needing You, loving You, taking strength from You, relying on You. People tell me I'm too hard on myself. Maybe I am. Maybe I'm not.

Lord, I want to confess my ugly sinful heart to You and lay it in front of You. My sin is so heavy, and You have promised to carry it. I don't want to ask You to carry it. I don't like asking for help…ever, especially when I can't repay it. But, Father, my sin is consuming me and breaking me and turning me callous and hollow.

I don't want to be shallow. I don't want my relationship with You to be empty and meaningless. Part of the reason I don't want that is because I want to look deep and spiritual to other people. I want people to say, "He really loves the Lord, and he is so sincere in his faith." Even this good thing of wanting to know You more and go deeper with You is tainted by the sin in me that wants to look good to others.

Lord, what do I do with that?

REGRETS **AND** GRACE

OREGON STATE

Sarah T.

We've all been there. You did it, and you knew you shouldn't have. All the same, though, we do it again the next time. Getting back with her, moving *beyond* with him, the show, the sex, the same situation again and again. Only to wake with shame and regrets. Deep regrets.

Why does this happen? Is it really how God wants us to live—rejected and hopeless due to our sin? I don't think so.

People always try to tell me all religions are the same. But there's something radically different about Christianity that *never* settles with that statement. It's summed up in a word: *grace.*

Not "if you do this, we'll do that" or "if you say this, you'll receive that." No, by definition, grace is a free gift.

"But because of his great love for us, God, who is rich in mercy, made us alive with Christ even when we were dead in transgressions—it is by grace you have been saved" (Ephesians 2:4–5). "When the kindness and love of God our Savior appeared, he saved us, not because of righteous things we had done, but because of his mercy" (Titus 3:4–5).

For some reason, though, we live at war with this promise. I do anyway. Aspects of guilt are holding me down today, and I hate it! It is blinding me from the freedom I know is there and paralyzing me from the freedom to really live at all.

College makes us do things we wouldn't normally do. Or at least *didn't* normally do. Whether it's the alcohol, environment, freedom, or exposure, I don't know, but for some reason, most people recount their most rebellious stories and regretful days as happening during college.

Okay, God doesn't expect us to be sinless. But He did call us to long for it, and to be honest and forthright in confessing our sins and accepting of the forgiveness He offers. Like any gift, grace requires an open hand, because a closed fist can't receive anything.

Maybe the best gift I can take from my campus is grace *received.*

SCHOOL OF **HARD** KNOCKS (SORTA)

SOUTHWEST MISSOURI STATE

Taylor S.

It was a late-night run to the grocery story. Caffeine hadn't delivered the buzz I needed. What I needed was something else, something to munch or drink or chew, something on the shelves down at the store. But when I got there, the place was locked up, or looked that way—doors closed, dark.

How could this be? I was desperate. I walked closer…only to be startled when the doors slid open.

Automatic doors do that.

So I walked in and bought what I wanted.

I've been thinking about those glass doors. Anyone would've assumed they were closed—because they were! But they're meant to open…if a person walks right up as if they *will* open.

I pass by a lot of closed doors—seemingly locked doors—in my life. Whether it's a decision here or a relationship there, I usually avoid what appears to be shut. But when I do that, the door itself isn't even my main problem. It's my reluctance to ask. It's my refusal to move past appearances or to believe in what I can't see.

Life can be lived passing what appears to be closed, or it can be lived putting faith in what will open. I'm trying to learn that God is the great Doorkeeper in my life. That doesn't mean He'll open every opportunity or desire I knock on. But if I knock in faith, He can and will open every good door.

I can count on that. And I can also count on the fact that pretty much every *un*-knocked-on door will remain closed!

We serve a huge God. We serve a God who not only opens doors, but who also dreams into our lives our desire to knock on them. For Him, nothing stands as necessarily closed. Ask your Father and trust He longs to give. Seek His face and believe He longs to seek back. Knock hard and surrender to the One who longs to open. "For everyone who asks receives; he who seeks finds; and to him who knocks, the door will be opened" (Matthew 7:8).

MY **BIGGEST** BATTLE

UCLA

Arunan A.

Okay, let me say it just to get it out in the open, because somebody needs to. All guys do struggle with, have struggled with, or will soon struggle with masturbation. In the culture we live in today, it's literally impossible to avoid. My pastor once told me he'd heard someone say, "Nine out of ten guys deal with masturbation, and the tenth one is a liar."

Actually, I think that's untrue—it's usually closer to four or five out of ten who lie about it, and in the Christian community, that number may rise to eight or nine out of ten who aren't really honest about it.

Every guy going into college needs to know this (because I definitely didn't know it when I was a freshman): You are not alone, so please don't be too ashamed to talk about it with others and get help. This is not a struggle you can handle on your own, so please don't try.

As with a lot of sins I'm learning to work through, masturbation is not the root cause of my struggle. It's just the endpoint in a series of struggles. It's usually sparked by images I see, or thoughts of me seeing them, which means that my biggest battle is guarding what I see and think about—especially when I'm alone.

Unfortunately, it's infinitely harder for guys to guard what we see than it was just ten or twenty years ago. There are sexually charged images all over TV, movies, and billboards. Just walking around a college campus on a summer day can set a guy off (girls, are you listening? Please watch what you wear, for our sakes). The Internet is obviously another huge player in all this, especially in the day of super-fast cable connections.

A couple of practical steps have really helped me.

1) There are a lot of great filter programs for your computer (I use X3 watch because it's free) that will make a log of all of the websites you go to and e-mail them to one or two accountability partners for you.

2) So what is an accountability partner? I didn't know what it was until I went to college. An accountability partner is simply someone who keeps you current on the truth about you, who keeps you current on where you need to be, and who can help you get up when you fall; it's someone you can be open, honest, and vulnerable with, someone who can help you walk through your issues. It's so important to have someone else involved in your inner life. Ecclesiastes 4:9–10 (NKJV) says, "Two are better than one...For if they fall, one will lift up his companion. But woe to him who is alone when he falls, for he has no one to help him up."

The most important thing, though, is that you have to get to your heart. If you want to deal with lust, you need to first deal with the way you look at the opposite sex. You have to *want* to deal with it before you can move forward. It's a tough battle, but God will always be bigger than anything we go up against. You don't have to be a slave to your sin. You don't have to let it shame you into detaching yourself from God or people. Be an open book before your friends and before God. That is the only way you can possibly combat lust. And, "It is for freedom that Christ set you free. Stand firm then, 'cause with Christ, you don't have to live in slavery to anything!" (Galatians 5:1, my paraphrase).

LUST IS A BRANCH

UNIVERSITY OF HOUSTON

Roy K.

The first fight for me was with semantics. We tend to be vague about the whole deal and say the easy words so it doesn't make our own skin crawl. "I have been struggling with lust" typically means "I have masturbated three times this week." One is just easier to say than the other.

But let's get closer to the truth: "I have had sex with myself three times this week." What does that do to you?

Those words could not make me feel any more wretched; the truth of the matter is that in this, I am wretched. We try to be vague, we try cop-outs like "every guy struggles with it" so we can be comforted in our transgressions. Well, guess what? You will never be comforted in your transgressions. We were not made that way. It has been a clanging symbol to the Lord in many a small group, where guys gather to confess their transgressions and leave saying, "Well, Tom and Mark both did it, too."

Maybe the whole small group movement tends to perpetuate the problem—like when we discuss things, but not in a holy manner. Or when we think addressing the issue is the same thing as really dealing with it—then go on sinning anyway.

How long have I struggled with lust (masturbation)? Since

I was 13. How long have I been a Christian? Since I was 8. The numbers just don't add up. Why is it that time and time again, I have the same confession on my heart?

Now, almost out of college, I can say the result of all my pondering, punching of pillows, and screams of anguish is that I've learned a few things. For example, when I get angry is when I struggle with lust the most. When I have had a hard, frustrating day, I'm more likely to reach for the temporal, shallow comfort lust brings. At those times, I find it harder to still my soul and address the real issue.

Because, in many ways, lust is *not* the real issue. It is a branch, along with a myriad of others, which receives its nourishment from roots that go deep into apathy, idleness, and unbelief. Addressing only lust is just trimming branches. I will continue to struggle with lust if I spend all my time focusing on only beating lust, so to speak.

Everything I could say by way of advice here sounds pretty "churchy." But I know deep down, when we really get a hold of God's Word on anything, nothing will suit us better. And I think He's speaking pretty directly to guys on this issue in Galatians 5:1 and 2:20–21, respectively. Eugene Peterson paraphrases these verses like this: "Christ has set us free to live a free life. So take your stand! Never again let anyone put a harness of slavery on you.... Indeed, I have been crucified with Christ. My ego is no longer central. It is no longer important that I appear righteous before you or have your good opinion, and I am no longer driven to impress God. Christ lives in me. The life you see me living is not 'mine,' but it is lived by faith in the Son of God, who loved me and gave himself for me. I am not going to go back on that" (*The Message*//Remix).

Chapter 5

THE GREEKS

G od could care less whether or not you rush, because kegs and Christianity (i.e., fraternities and faith) have nothing in common.

Both false—at least based on what I see in the Bible or hear from students on various campuses. God *is* interested in whether or not you rush, because He cares greatly about the keg/Christianity scene.

There is nothing inherently "bad" about joining a fraternity or sorority. I've witnessed radical transformations and major degradations in both. Call me a heathen, but I think Greek life often displays a more biblical embrace of community than most churches.

Of course, God doesn't *need* you to accomplish anything, but He *chooses* you to accomplish a lot—to weave your little life into His big one. I love Tyler's description of looking back on his time in a frat house:

"I can't even come close to explaining how much I learned throughout the year. God was so faithful. There wasn't a day when I felt fully adequate, but I was con-tinually renewed and kept remembering that God hadn't asked me to be adequate. He had simply called out my name and allowed me the chance to respond."

Maybe God is leading you to live at home or in a dorm or apartment. Then again, maybe He's inviting you to spend the next season of your life in the middle of the Greek scene.

Different choices, same huge God. Delta Zeta or Kappa Delta, His name remains Alpha and Omega.

—abbie

"Commit to the LORD whatever you do,
and your plans will succeed."

PROVERBS 16:3

HOTEL CHECK-IN

GEORGIA TECH

Clay S.

G rowing up in a Christian home is a gift that should never be taken for granted. I will always be thankful for this "head start" God gave me. I believe my relationship with Him is so much more intimate and mature than it would have been otherwise. I grew up with a family and a church that encouraged me to spend time with my Creator. With this blessing, however, also comes a lot of naiveté. Even though I went to a large, inner city, public high school, I still didn't realize that sex and drugs would be so "normal" and commonplace in college.

With this in mind, you can understand my shock when I arrived at the Miami Radisson Hotel for my first fraternity formal.

"Hi. We're the fraternity from Georgia Tech here to check in."

"What is your name?" the desk clerk kindly responded.

"Oh yeah, I'm Clay, and this is my date Kelly. My friend, Matt, will be in my room, and Kelly and his date will take another," I explained and then turned to make conversation with my date. At the door, some other guys from our fraternity started rolling in.

"What's up, guys? How was the trip?" I asked, as the alcohol stench of my not-so-well-mannered brothers quickly spread throughout the lobby.

"Good, man, and we're headed out to the pool to kick the keg before cocktail hour. Come on out when you're done here!"

A little embarrassed, I turned back to the hotel clerk as she politely said, "I'm sorry, sir, but we don't have a separate room for your date. Your room is showing up, but it's a room for four, not two."

A little taken aback, I turned to our fraternity's treasurer and explained that I had signed up for a double room. He just laughed and said, "A double room means one bed for you and your date and one for Matt and his date. Sweet!"

"One room for the four of us?" I asked.

That had to be wrong. Was he saying that everyone would stay alone in a room with their dates? Did I miss a Sunday school class where this Bible story was explained?

Our fraternity is definitely a social fraternity, but there is also a fairly strong Christian influence, which is what had attracted me to it four months earlier, during rush. We had about ten guys who were fairly outspoken Christians and (I thought) had a strong degree of morality. But I was shocked to find that this weekend, even they had planned to sleep in the same beds with their girlfriends or dates. Speechless and embarrassed, I quickly grabbed the key from the hotel clerk, picked up my bags, and scurried to find our rooms.

After everyone had settled in, we made our way down to the pool deck, with blaring music and numerous tapped kegs.

Regardless of the good weather and company, my mind was stuck on the awkwardness of spending that night in the same bed with another girl. Maybe we could do guys in one bed, girls in the other. Or what about guys on the floor? But how would we all get dressed for the formal? Matt and me in the bathroom? No, the girls needed the bathroom. This sucked.

The same question kept running through my mind: How could all these Christian guys, who I had so much respect for, sleep in the same beds with their dates? It seemed like at least one of them would have opted for different rooms? When I asked around, though, none of the Christian guys had even given a second thought to the option of separate rooms. It just seemed normal, they said, that at a formal, you sleep with your date. Not necessarily have sex with her, but just sleep in the same bed.

Right.

I was honestly ready to cave into the pressure, when out of the blue, one of my brothers yelled, "Hey, Clay, some bus that says the name of your town is outside."

There was no way. My hometown is small. I was the only one in my fraternity from Granville, and there were only three of us from Alabama. As I went through the lobby, though, I was shocked and ecstatic to see my church's tacky van parked outside. Getting closer, I saw twenty-five familiar faces. I felt like a war hero returning home. They found my being at the fraternity formal pretty amusing, as they'd just returned from a prayer time in which they mentioned the lost people partying at the nearby pool!

Anyway, after explaining the situation, my old youth pastor was quick to point out that they had an extra room from someone dropping out at the last minute. Without a second thought, I claimed that room for Kelly and Matt's date, and we stayed in the double. That night was by far one of the best nights of sleep I've ever had—alone and in a bed by myself.

It's so easy to cave into pressure. "No one will know, everyone is doing it, and God will surely understand, because there are no other options." I was tempted by every one of these justifications that weekend, and I was certainly ready to count out God. Thankfully, though, He wasn't ready to count out me. God intervened in a miraculous way and gave me a wonderful opportunity to obey Him.

YOU **MUST** HAVE
THE WRONG **GUY**

EMORY UNIVERSITY

Tyler S.

G od, You've got to be joking. This is not a job I'm capable of. I'm going to be so in over my head. I'm not nearly equipped for work like this. I don't have enough knowledge. Lord, it scares me to death that You would put me in this situation—You clearly don't know me well enough."

Does this sound familiar? Have you ever wondered what God was doing, or why He orchestrated a given situation like He did? Well, this was exactly where I was my junior year when several guys I really respected asked me to run for president of our fraternity. There are a couple things to keep in mind here: When I pledged and joined the fraternity, I partied and carried on like any other frat guy. Then, during the summer after my freshman year, God opened my eyes to how temporal all of the things I had been putting my faith in truly were, and it changed me.

So, everyone in the fraternity thought they were getting one guy, and it turned out they got another one. I, too, thought I was getting a group of friends that I could really relate to and enjoy, and I ended up getting friends who were focused on everything that I wasn't really all that interested in. For me to lead a group of nearly a hundred guys with totally different priorities and beliefs than me didn't make any sense. I thought I was playing the role God had for me by serving on our college ministry's servant leadership team. God had a different story. Thankfully, the story He wanted me in was much better than the one I had planned out.

One thing led to the next, and before I knew it, I was making the acceptance speech in front of the entire chapter. I gradually got excited about the whole deal, but was still convinced that God had somehow mistaken me with another person. As the year went on, though, I began to see His footprints and realized more and more how blessed I was to be a tool within these imprints. He didn't need me to do anything unbelievable or miraculous. He just needed me to stand obedient to His calling, to plant the seeds, and to allow Him to work His wonders. Years ago my pastor had said, "Do the things that you know will make you look like an idiot if you fail. This is when you really get to see God go to work." But it wasn't until this experience that I caught a glimpse of the true significance of this.

Putting the whole experience into words would be tough, but imagine babysitting a hundred eighteen- to twenty-one-year olds who think they own the world. This is not an exaggeration. My schedule was full of board meetings, house sessions, and interfraternity sessions. The fun part was the not-so-planned events, like intervening between a bunch of testosterone-fueled guys throwing bottles at each other between houses. Or getting a rally call for protection for a brother who was being chased because he had been at a bar, hitting on some other frat's girl.

Oh, I almost forgot the trip to the county jail to bail someone out for getting rowdy with a police officer.

Even with all these events, I can't even come close to explaining how much I learned throughout the year—for example, the difference between personal principles and collective ethics, or how to lead in everyday situations. God was so faithful in allowing me to lean on Him and not feel the burden of serving on my own. There wasn't a day when I felt fully adequate, but I was continually renewed and kept remembering that God hadn't asked me to be adequate. He had simply called out my name and allowed me the chance to respond.

Our house still isn't sober, and every guy certainly isn't a believer. But I do see ripple effects. I even see tangible fruit, and I can only wonder about the seeds that have been sown and are still to sprout. You never know how many apples will eventually result from one seed.

BONGS IN **CHURCH**

Texas A&M University

Allison W.

I love my sorority and the ways it's impacted my life these past two years, but when I heard about our annual carnival taking place in my church, I wasn't thrilled. Maybe I'm too conservative, but churchy things are for the church, and "other things" are for other places. And knowing the crowd that would come, I can't exactly say the "holiness barometer" was going to be soaring.

I refused to be on the planning committee, but was still required to attend the event. Being quite the pessimist, I envisioned torn-down icons and smashed crucifixes decorating the floor. Though it wasn't quite this extreme, it still didn't cut the Sunday morning vibe. Entering through the front sanctuary, I felt like I'd entered a circus on steroids—music, games, two kegs, too many bongs to count...all unraveling in a house of God. Tears welled up in my eyes as I struggled to maintain composure. We were mocking God to His face. Not to be overspiritualizing, but I couldn't help but get a sense of what Jesus must have felt walking into the temple. No wonder He was so angry.

With everything spinning around me, I got stuck in a trance staring at a small carving near the front of the room. It was Jesus. Not a Jesus who was siding with me or feeling sorry for my situation, but a Jesus who was looking down and feeling sorry for *me*. In a matter of minutes (it seemed like hours), He took me inward and allowed me to stop obsessing about the outward. My sorority was enveloped by sin, no question. But the more pressing question suddenly became, "What are the deeply rooted carnivals going on in *your* soul?" It was as if God was saying, "Your heart is one big, orgiastic carnival, too." Again, in a matter of minutes, God had taken a terribly disturbing circumstance around me and challenged me right back with the terribly disturbing circumstance inside me.

I left the carnival that day, or at least the one in the church. But that experience was the beginning of a peeling back, a journey to the state of my heart. I was tired of the superficial Christian I had become. I was tired of the pretty, heart-shaped box that had taken the place of real faith.

If they let me, I've decided to volunteer for the planning team next year. And I'll probably suggest doing the carnival at the church.

GOD, I'LL
GET BACK TO YOU

University of North Carolina

Nick J.

My senior year of high school came with college applications, acceptance letters, and senioritis at maximum force. I was anxious for the escape and freedom of living away from home. As with many high school students, I had experimented with drinking, so I could imagine the fun nights it would create in college. The next four years would be one big party.

My freshman year of college turned out to be all that and more—parties, girls, beer, pot, and all the freedom I'd ever dreamed of! I was making a bunch of friends and meeting twice as many girls. I gloated in the fact that I went from being the adolescent dork to one of the guys everyone had heard of. I joined a fraternity my second semester so I could have more parties to go to. Classes got pushed aside, and I rationalized my low GPA to my parents by saying school was just harder than I expected.

The continuous party life carried on for the next two years. My grades improved a bit, but so did my tolerance for alcohol, marijuana, and girls. I was wandering in this party and hook-up culture, and, I'm not gonna lie, these things brought me happiness. But it didn't last.

Up to that point in my life, I definitely would have told you that I was a Christian. I knew there was a God and even believed that Jesus died on the cross. College just seemed like a time when it was okay to put God in the background. It was like saying, "God, I know You're there, but You know, I'm just having too much fun right now. If I start listening to You, life will be boring, so just give me some time and I'll get back to You. In fact, just give me two more years of fun, and then I'll be a better person."

During my senior year, God's gentle knock started to get a little louder. (It had probably always been loud, and I was just too distracted to hear it.) I had come to a point where, although I was still partying a lot, I realized that the parties weren't as much fun anymore. We'd get trashed, do stupid things with anything or anyone, and then wake up in the afternoon of the next day wondering what had happened.

About this time, one of my fraternity brothers asked if I'd like to be in his Bible study. Because partying had started to wear on me, I decided maybe it would be a good idea. Six of us started meeting on a weekly basis, and before long, I found myself looking forward to our study.

Not long after, the brother who was leading our Bible study invited me to a nationwide, Christian, Greek Conference in Indiana. I knew I wouldn't fit in and honestly wasn't thrilled about the idea of hanging out with a bunch of real (i.e., boring) Christians. I pictured a long, drawn-out weekend that would leave me feeling nothing but more guilty. But deep down, I was honestly just scared. I was scared that God was going to expose my sin to all those people. At the same time, I was scared that He was going to make me into a holy person who never had fun.

With some encouragement, however, I finally decided to go. The conference started off with a time of worship through music. This was something I had never really done before. I had always sung from a torn, dusty hymnal backed by a struggling choir and an out-of-tune organ. This band was actually good. I'll admit, however, I was a little weirded out when people started raising their hands and closing their eyes to sing.

Saturday night of the retreat, we had an '80s dance music party, which was boring and convicting at the same time. I realized that I couldn't have fun anymore without being drunk. I couldn't dance unless I had at least a twelve pack in me.

During the next morning session, I was beginning to realize that something in me was yearning for change, but I wasn't quite ready to verbalize this. During worship, I tried to focus on the words of the songs, as opposed to just singing them. In fact, I even tried closing my eyes. I was shocked at how the speakers that day seemed to be talking directly to me. It was as if God had prompted them to give a message focused on my life alone.

The conference ended with students from different Greek chapters all over the country sharing how God had revealed Himself throughout the weekend. These few minutes changed my life in a radical way. It hit me that this God figure was a whole lot bigger than just a man who died for me. Every single student at the conference had felt His power and overwhelming presence that weekend. For me, that seemed unbelievable! There wasn't a question in my mind, from that point onward, that I needed to make some major investments in my understandings of God. I realized that there was so much more to me being a

Christian than just knowing that there was a God (even Satan knew that!). He actually wanted an intimate relationship with me—a messed up, selfish, confused, prideful, insecure nobody. One of the Scriptures that really spoke to me was 2 Corinthians 5:17: "Therefore, if anyone is in Christ, he is a new creation; the old has gone, the new has come!" I could honestly feel new life being born in me and was no longer scared, but strangely excited. I felt truly alive and free for the first time.

My Christian fraternity brother began discipling me, and I got involved in a church near our campus. I remained full of questions and far from understanding God, but I realized that that didn't matter. I accepted that God knew all of me. One of the most important things I've come to realize is that the life I was afraid to give up was not all what I thought it was. And the life that I was scared to have—the so-called boring, rule-driven life—is so much more fulfilling and exciting with Christ setting the pace. I was no longer experiencing mere passing happiness, but joy.

Chapter 6

DATING

I am sick of conversations about dating. What's right, what's wrong. What's fun and okay, what's going too far. There are enough ongoing debates to drive anyone crazy. Don't get me wrong—I'm a huge fan of the guy/girl stuff. I also don't think broken hearts and scarred relationships always have to be your conclusion.

As the coming pages testify, relationships are messy—dating or otherwise. Whether you're struggling in singleness, sulking in heartbreak, or steering toward the altar, there's no easy solution. But there is a way through.

Reality is, God formed the lightning bolts, so give Him some credit on the *who* and *when* aspects of your love life. It's easy to assume that a little PR on your behalf (cute jeans or a pimped-out car) is necessary. Probably not. Who you are is how God made you today. Accept it. Any "should be" is culture's whisper and every "if only" is doubt saying God's not in control.

Whether what you hope for is simple friendship or a courtship, God knows what you want before you want it. The command is to "delight yourselves in the LORD," and the promise is that "He will give you the desires of your heart"

(Psalm 37:4). It's an unbelievable verse, but we too often settle for just the latter half.

God knows you. He's enthralled by you. And to the extent of death, He wants you to experience love.

—abbie

I will instruct you and teach you in the way you should go;
I will counsel you and watch over you.

PSALM 32:8

BOUNDARIES

Baylor University

John M.

O ne thing there's plenty of in college is dating advice. Everybody seems to have their own theories, and they all want to share them with you. On top of all the personal advice, there's a plethora of books taking a variety of approaches. When should you start dating? What should dating look like? How serious should it be?

My favorite topic is boundaries, mainly because it's comical listening to people talk about it. Before I got to college, I'd never heard the word "boundaries," but I can't even count the amount of conversations I had about it within a few weeks of joining a Christian group. I was once at a Christian bookstore where I noticed a whole shelf full of books on where to set boundaries in various situations. I didn't read any of them, but I can guess what they all said. I wanted to (in response) write a book called *Boundaries Suck: How We've Used Laws to Cut God Out of the Church*, and I started on it, until I realized I would probably be hung or stoned by Christians if the book ever got published.

Many people feel that if they follow the boundaries the Church has given regarding relationships and lust, then they'll be okay. But often our boundaries are man-made attempts to try to control the situation, instead of putting it in God's hands. The clearest evidence of that is the fact that we all have different boundaries. I asked a bunch of my Christian friends: "At what exact moment in the series of events that lead up to him sleeping with Bathsheba and killing her husband did King David actually commit a sin?" I got nothing close to a consensus. Instead, I got pretty much every answer ranging from the fact that he was home from the war, to he was looking at her for the first time, to the first kiss, to sleeping with her, to killing her husband. But the most common response was, people would think about it for a while and say, "I have no idea."

Boundaries are easy for us as Christians because they're very two-dimensional, straightforward, black-and-white, a definite line that you are allowed to go right up to the edge of, but not cross over. Boundaries are the slippery slope that leads toward the edge of a cliff. A sensible person would stay as far back from the cliff as they can, instead of seeing how close they can get, just for the heck of it. Sometimes it's great because it affords us a glimpse of a grand view, some amount of pleasure, but it can lead to a fall and a lot of brokenness.

I remember talking to a Christian friend of mine who confided in me that she had recently lost her virginity. She was lamenting that she felt she was no longer pure, and that no good guy would want her anymore because she was "damaged goods." The church had convinced her that she could go to a certain line with no guilt, but once she crossed it, she was no longer pure. I said that purity is not about virginity; it is a condition of the heart. David had an adulterous relationship (one in which both he and the woman were married), and then murdered the woman's husband, and he was still considered "the man after God's own heart."

The act of sex is not the point; a pure heart is. God judges your heart, not your history, and no matter what people think or say, it's only His judgment that counts. I'm not saying that this justifies a sexual carte blanche, but rather that Christians are a bit mixed up when they try to change their actions instead of changing their hearts. The whole point of Jesus' message to the Pharisees was that God doesn't judge on our outer appearance, but on our inner being.

RANDOM
THOUGHTS ON A&E

EMORY UNIVERSITY

Tyler S.

Dear Friend~
You were created from Adam's rib, not from dust
like man and Adam said
"Whoa-man!" You're beautiful. (This isn't my
point in writing, but wanted to remind you). My point
is to say God created you and I in His likeness and in
the beginning God walked in the Garden with Adam and
Eve. We were created and were in the presence of God.
Have you ever thought about the significance of this?
I have. Let me begin to tell you what it means and
then I have to finish typing up my paper and go share
the gospel of Christ to someone who I think is going
to become a Christian tonight.
God's about to drop the straight G-Bomb on this kid and I get to
participate! There's no word strong enough for the
excitement that brings me...while not appropriate, it
almost makes me want to say "[expletive] yeah!" So
hard to describe the feeling of a soul being

saved in two words. We don't have any strong enough—
guess that's why people use poetry and stuff.
Sidetracked, sorry. Anyway, the point is that Adam
and Eve were in the presence of God in the Garden.
That's not very unusual if it was a fairytale—"Huh,
A & E were in the same place as God…? No biggie."
WRONG. Huge. This means that they were sinless,
guiltless beings who were WORTHY of being in the
presence of God, who was never created and will never
cease to exist! Again, that's the mind-blowing stuff
that makes me want to drop another expletive. They
were in the presence of God and He didn't have to
dress Himself up as a bush, or send an angel, or kill
them because they were in His presence. Wow. Have
I said that part yet?
I don't think I'm capturing this. They were created
with God's Glory beaming out from them. They were
created shining the beauty of God like a HUGE mirror
reflecting the sun's rays. The mirror was the size of
a tennis court, being held up by a huge stand so that
it would reflect God's glory on earth. Just outta-
control brightness…Man, imagine the brilliance we
were created with…God created us like that and
wanted intimacy with us…In fact, He had such
intimacy with us that we didn't have any clothes on
and He could walk right up to us and relate to us. If
you can't imagine that, it's because of all the sin
blocking your mind. He created us with the purpose to
reflect His Glory better than anything else He made.
That's why He keeps pursuing us. We're the only ones

made in His image.

BUT, and this is a big BUT…

A & E took that HUGE mirror, like the size of a tennis
court again, being held up by a huge stand, and they BUSTED
it…it shattered all over the place. Makes me
wanna swear again.

%*#$!

Why did they do that? "'Cause God is sovereign…"
Doesn't do it for me…I just can't understand…
It's beyond me.

Point is that if you start the gospel at "all have
sinned and fall short of the glory of God" (Romans 3:23)
you miss the whole story. God didn't create us WITH
SIN. He created us WITHOUT SIN. It's not part of us,
we just chose to add it because we thought we could
create something better.

Remember the GLORY you were created for. Don't
forget it. Satan's going to try to cloud it out by
sin and all of the bull around you. He's going to
cloud it out because it doesn't look like God's
working…if God's not working He's gone and if He's
gone He doesn't love you. He does love you. In fact,
He can't help but be in your life because He loves you
so much. Every time His justice tells Him to walk
away, His love tells Him, "YOU HAVE NO CHOICE." Please
understand, God is limited by His character.

Thankfully, 1 John is right. God is LOVE (1 John
4:8b, 16) and God is, therefore, limited by the fact
that He is hopelessly in love with us. So much so
that He couldn't help but slaughter His own Son to

gain a relationship with us. He couldn't help Himself
because of who He is.

When you feel like you need a husband or a wife, remember
that

there's one person who knows you better than anyone else,
and has pursued you to the ends of the earth: God.
He's crazy about you. So crazy about you, the things
He does for you aren't even logical. So crazy about
you, He keeps pursuing you even though you act
like you hate Him. Even though you don't return His
calls. Even though you ignore His love letters. Even
though He sent His Son to teach you about how much He
loves you, and you killed Him. Even though every day,
when you wake up, He's been waiting through the night
to pursue you again. In fact, sometimes He doesn't
even wait. Man does He love you.

attempting to love,

Tyler

THAT **CRAZY** CHRISTIAN DATING **BOOK**

Texas A&M University

Becky L.

I was not exactly happy to see Tom in my math class that first day of fall semester. We'd played intramural soccer together and I knew of him from our campus ministry, but I certainly couldn't deal with the pressure of having him in one of my classes. Everyone would say how nice Tom was and what a great person he seemed to be, but these were moot points to me, in light of his appearance. All I could see was how incredibly cute his face was and toned his biceps were. He was tall and blond, model material no doubt, and I couldn't help but blush at the very thought of him. I was obsessed, to say the least, and practically nonfunctional when around him. Therefore, seeing him in my math class was not exactly a good thing. All I could imagine was day after day of embarrassing moments and ineptness on my part whenever I saw him.

I managed to avoid his detection that first day of class, but the secret was let out that afternoon at intramural soccer practice. But actually, after that first conversation, we began to have some "normal" conversations. Class actually became something

I looked forward to as we slowly developed a completely unexpected friendship. I went to a few of his basketball games, which were often followed by going out for ice cream or coffee.

I spoke about Tom endlessly to my friends, giving them every detail of all he said or did. Having a guy, a cute guy at that, pursue me was so exciting! I'd never had a boyfriend before or even dated. Our time together became exclusive pretty fast, and by finals, our "study" sessions were nothing more than physical fun and cuddling.

After Christmas break, our physical relationship moved along quite fast. It was at this point when I first questioned what being a Christian meant in relation to dating Tom. A godly woman friend explained that there are guidelines for a healthy, Christ-glorifying relationship. I eagerly read a book she gave me. I finished it in about three hours, and wrote it off in about three minutes! I thought Tom's and my relationship reflected what it said, like making the physical, emotional, and spiritual aspects grow slowly, as well as keeping communication lines open and honest. I agreed that God needed to remain the center of any dating relationship, but I was turned off by too many hyperstrict rules, which in my opinion, no dating couple would ever conceive of following (no passionate kissing?!). In a lot of ways, I desired, and felt the need, to make up for my "lost time" of not dating in high school. At this point, because I didn't have strong Christian friends, I was constantly comparing myself to non-Christians or our culture's guidelines for dating. I had never wanted to have sex before marriage, but I thought anything apart from that was fine. Besides, Tom and I had met in the context of a Christian group, so I had no doubts that we were practicing a "Christian relationship."

It didn't occur to me to pray about our relationship, and we certainly never talked about God. I actually wanted to, but I was afraid that a "deep" conversation might ruin things. I was still so in awe that someone liked me. Although Tom's attendance at our campus Christian events seemed to be decreasing, I compensated for that fact by believing that his occasional volunteer projects were proof enough of his faith.

Honestly, I didn't realize how sinful our relationship was until after we broke up. The split obviously surprised me, as I really had no idea anything was wrong. After Tom broke up with me, I was more confused than anything—confused as to what went wrong, what had happened between us, and what it meant now that things were over.

During this time, I was selected to be on our ministry's leadership team. This obviously meant spending a lot of time with our staff workers, a young and enthusiastic married couple. A foreign, yet totally intriguing, aspect of their relationship that drew me to it was God's integral role in every aspect of it. I had always called myself a Christian, though it wasn't until now that I realized being a Christian meant having a daily, living relationship with God. I realized how I'd separated my dating relationship from my identity as a Christian. I believed in God and talked about being a Christian throughout those months with Tom, but the problem was, it was the same way I would talk about being a sociology major, or someone who loves sports. I also realized that the relationship had been sexually sinful, even though we hadn't had sex. Because it was sinful, that meant I was a sinner. I know this sounds obvious, but it was something I had never taken to heart or truly internalized. I knew Jesus died for my sins, though really never thought of, or admitted to, having a sin big enough that would require His death. But during this time, I saw that to God, sin is sin, no matter what it is, and all He asks is that we repent of it. Romans 3:23–24 says, "For all have sinned and fall short of the glory of God"...and then the best part..."and are justified freely by his grace through the redemption that came by Christ Jesus."

I realize now that I went through the motions of trying to have a Christian relationship. But I never knew what these motions should be. I never prayed or sought God's will for the relationship, let alone my life. I don't regret that stage of my life, because I know the experience was God's way of teaching me about my need for a Savior and His unending love for and pursuit of me. My relationship with God actually became better because of a bad relationship with a guy, and for that I couldn't be more thankful! And about that book on Christian dating, well, I don't think it's so crazy anymore. I've even read a few more!

DON'T **DATE** YOUR **FIRST** SEMESTER

AMERICAN UNIVERSITY

Amy G.

D on't date your first semester." Ten people probably told me this before I left for school. But my freshman year began, and I might've been the first to have a boyfriend. I'm not superdependent on people, and I don't have a singleness complex, but dating is fun—and with a whole new pool in front of me, I figured, "What the heck!" My faith was in line, and I wasn't about to think some guy could distract that. Endless time together (and endless IMs and texts when we weren't together) could be justified by the new environment. About halfway through the year, though, with a broken heart and seemingly broken connection with God, I realized the advice might have been given for good reason.

It's easy to fall in love with what we see. It's right there. Sucks that "seeing" and "right there" can just as quickly become unseen and gone. Does anything last? Is anything trustworthy? Jesus says we can't serve two masters (Matthew 6:24). It doesn't matter if that master is a boyfriend/job/boss/identity/sport—it can't compete with Him. That answer tends to make me mad.

I don't want to serve a God who can do anything in a matter of seconds or who demands everything from me. But I also don't want to believe in a God who can't or doesn't.

I guess I could say it would've been better if I didn't date that first semester. I'd have a lot prettier story to tell, in a more polished Christianese accent. But that's not what happened. That's not my story. I was given good advice and decided not to take it. Do I regret that? Kind of. I realize that it happened, and the question is now, How will I move forward from here? Because I certainly can't and wouldn't give back what I learned first semester. I might take advice a little more seriously, or dating a little less frivolously, but if God is really who He says He is, He's in control. He knows what happened, and I think His greatest concern is what I will do now and how I will grow from that happening.

WEIRD THEORIES VS. REAL LIFE

COLORADO UNIVERSITY,

Jonathan A.

Michelle and I had dated all through high school and were determined to stay together when we went off to college. We'd had our rough times (and expected many more to come), but overall, had a very pure and what we considered "godly" relationship. Nobody else was too encouraging of our plan. They gave us the typical lines of, "You're not mature enough," or, "Maybe you need some time apart," or, "Visiting each others' campuses will make you miss what's on your own." By the time we left, they were at least "supportive of what we decided."

Being four hours apart was hard, but I guess like anything else, we just tried to trust God that we were doing what He wanted. Freshman year was the hardest. Michelle rushed a sorority, and I got really involved with our campus ministry. We found ourselves arguing on the phone a lot and trying to sort through things that seemed really stupid. Plus, living on a hall full of brash, drunken guys didn't always help my phone focusability, if that's a word. When we'd finally get to see each other, things were really good. Sometimes the physical temptations were harder, just because we'd been apart for a while, but overall, we stayed on the same page about continuing to date.

Michelle and I had always attended the same church, so we had essentially watched the other grow up. For some reason, though, it was easier to see, or at least recognize, process from a distance. I'm not going to bore you with details (Michelle said the girls would actually like them, though); I will say we've stayed together for three and a half years and plan to graduate this spring and then to marry in August.

I feel like I'm trying to accomplish a lot in this short entry of a book. I guess if I had to make a statement of a point, though, or come to some essence of "what I've learned," it's that God really is the Author of our faith. He's the Author of chapters and segments, but also periods and spaces. Sometimes He/they make sense, but probably more times they don't. Sometimes people will agree, or advise, and other times they won't. When all is said and done, I think there's something deep in you that knows what's really right. You don't have to avoid dating, and you don't have to date everyone who crosses your path. You don't have to figure out if *he's the one* before the check's even been paid, but you also don't need to wait for Jesus Jr. before going out for coffee. I'll shut up now.

This whole Christian dating thing just really gets me fired up. There's so much about it that just seems so weird. There are a lot of theories about how Christian relationships *could* work. But I think for Michelle and me, the biggest thing was realizing God is the only one who knows how they *should* work. Formulas are great, but in the end, you're not going to discover your life partner by an explanation in a book. Follow God with everything you've got and trust that if He keeps doing things like He's done for ALL generations, He'll lead you to rich waters.

FIRE **DRILL**

MINNESOTA COLLEGE

Brett B.

Katie and I started dating the spring of my sophomore year. We were introduced through a mutual friend on campus. Both of us were grounded in our faith and felt confident about glorifying God in the context of dating. We stayed together into our junior year, when I became the RA of a freshman dorm. This role opened my eyes to a lot of new responsibility, but a lot of new respect, too. As for Katie and me, we tried to keep our relationship outside the dorm doors, but I was pretty open and figured the influence of healthy dating might rub off on them. They knew we weren't having sex, and I tried to be as honest as I could about guarding hearts, boundaries, etc.

A lot of nights were spent studying late, and Katie would end up staying in my room, her on the bed and me the futon. Never a second thought.

Until the fire alarm went off one night at 3 a.m. It was the middle of exams, of course. I'd normally sleep through an obnoxious/obviously false alarm like this, but that's a negative bit to the RA thing. Katie got this astonished look on her face and said, "We can't walk out of here together! Do you know what that looks like?"

That's silly…people knew us and knew how "Christian" we were, especially in the stance of not sleeping together. But who *wouldn't* assume stuff when we're even walking out of the bedroom in our pajamas? You could give me Mr. and Mrs. Christian, and I'd tell you that setup assumed nothing *but* sex.

The only thing people knew was that I was supposed to be some model guy who liked God and my girlfriend. They didn't know I slept on the futon. They didn't know we hadn't even kissed, let alone had sex. And even if the guys on my hall didn't think stuff, what about the other three hundred residents? What about guys in our campus ministry, who merely knew me as the upperclassman who did announcements every Wednesday night?

Or the other RAs, who'd known me for three years as the "trustworthy Christian"? How would they view this? Uhhhh… we never intended to give this impression.

Something I realized through this experience is that we can make a lot of things easier. Katie didn't *need* to sleep in my dorm. You could take it to another level and say we didn't *need* to be up that late in the first place, but whatever. Her sleeping in my dorm saved us a lot of time and energy. But what I'm learning is that bringing ease to my life isn't always the best decision. We don't call ourselves Christians because it makes life easier; it usually makes it harder. We have been called to live *in* the world, but not *of* the world. I wanted to write an explanatory e-mail to the entire dorm that night, but that wasn't very rational or maybe even practical. After our three-minute assessment, which seemed like three years of agony, we decided we needed to go outside— not for confession, but because a) there was a fire alarm, and b) what was done was done.

We couldn't change it, but at least we could learn from it for future nights.

We never heard anything more about the fire alarm that night, or why I walked out with Katie. But I realize now that doesn't even matter. As much as we get caught thinking otherwise, being a Christian is not based on what's said, not said, or assumed by other people. We're accountable to God first. Nonetheless, I'll sure as heck never do it again; it was truly God's timing that led us to repentance that night. Aside from not sleeping in my room together anymore, we also became more certain that God really is all about love and open arms (and random setups) to get us back to Him.

FREED **AND** FORGIVEN

UNIVERSITY OF NORTH FLORIDA

Ryan T.

I would be the last person you'd expect to write about dating in a Christian book. I professed a faith in Jesus Christ over ten years ago, but I have just recently begun to live my life that way. There's no reason for details, but let's just say my dating and sexual life has been far from pure. I began experimenting with sex when I was thirteen. I've been to strip joints, experimented with drugs and bisexuality, and even been in an adulterous relationship. Am I proud of any one of these things? Far from it. But is there anything I can do to change where I've been? No. The only thing I can do is change where I'm going.

This was the changer for me—literally, spending time with this verse has changed my life: "God's kindness leads you toward repentance" (Romans 2:4). I always thought the opposite.

As I write this, am I still embarrassed about my past? Yes. But I'm not going to let my failures leave me separated from a life of love and certainly a life of loving God. There is nothing bigger than the cross of Jesus Christ—not in my past and not in my future. "Therefore, there is now no condemnation for those who are in Christ Jesus, because through Christ Jesus the law of the Spirit of life set me free from the law of sin and death" (Romans 8:1–2).

Chapter 7

OUTSIDE
THE **CLASSROOM**

C ollege has far more education to offer than just what's
reflected by a GPA and diploma. In fact, I'm willing to bet
that more learning occurs outside the classroom than inside.

If you have an interest or a hobby, there's a group that does
it. If there's not one, you can create it. Sounds crazy, but you
can literally do whatever you want. No one will stop you, and
in most cases, few will even challenge you.

Specific to faith, most campuses offer an array of worship
options. And again, if they don't, gather two or more and expect
God to show up. My encouragement is this: Do anything but
become a Christian hermit or clone. God doesn't need minds
that think the same or hearts that love the same. Bottom line—
get outside your box.

Sometimes it takes effort to connect with people who are
unlike us. I guess because it takes focusing on someone other
than ourselves. As Courtney relates in one of the following entries,
"College is possibly the most selfish and self-absorbed time of
one's life. Almost by default, everything is always about *me* (my

schedule, my job, my grades, my social life, my sleep, my dating)."

I'm not saying avoid campus ministries or your local church. Far from it! You need fellowship and accountability to survive. But I'm convinced there's more. Not only does Jesus straight up say so (Mark 2:17; Matthew 9:12), but He does so (entire New Testament). Christ prioritized time with believers, but also spent loads of time with unbelievers. Hung on a cross for them, too.

—abbie

I thank Christ Jesus our Lord,
who has given me strength,
that he considered me faithful,
appointing me to his service.
1 TIMOTHY 1:12

GO WITH THE FLOW

UCLA

Arunan A.

When I started college, I felt almost overwhelmed by the number of fellowships and Christian events that were available. But I was a Christian, and I wanted to do the whole "Christian thing" (because I felt that is what I should do), so I tried to take them all in. It was like a giant buffet, and just like every good buffet for a college student, the quantity mattered more than the quality. At one point, I was literally at some kind of Christian event every single night of the week.

Actually, they all pretty much looked the same: A dude gets up with a guitar and sings some songs, then some other dude comes up with a Bible and preaches, and then we go home.

In the beginning I just sat in the back and took it all in. I thought the point of these fellowships was to soak it all up so I could be more wise or spiritual or something, but soon I felt really frustrated. I felt like I wasn't growing, like I wasn't connecting to God. I didn't understand the problem. I was coming to Christian events regularly; shouldn't that be enough? I finally asked one of the Campus Crusade leaders, and he said that was the exact problem.

When you try to "soak up God" without serving others, you will eventually reach a saturation point. A lake can only receive a certain amount of water if it has no outlet, but a river has constant water flowing through it. In the same way, we, as Christians, are made to have new water flow into us only if it is flowing out of us to others. So where is God working, and how does He want me to flow? God only works toward the things that are eternal, and only two things on earth are eternal: God Himself and people. We need to invest in God (I always got that part), but we also need to invest in people (that's what I missed).

Everything we do in life should be in some way geared toward one of those two things. While He was on earth, Christ invested His time mainly with individuals. His ministry was largely unsuccessful from a worldly view (after his death, Acts records only 120 followers of Christ), but because of the *quality* of this investment, the whole world was changed through those 120 people. If Christ tried to start a megachurch of the sort that Christians love so much today, His revolutionary movement would have probably died out long ago.

God made us for interaction with others and with Him, and it's the most rewarding thing you can do with your life. Don't let your college career go by and be just about academics, or extracurriculars, or whatever. Let it be about the relationships you build and the lives you impact.

A **LIGHT** NEEDS A **SOURCE**

CORNELL UNIVERSITY

Michelle S.

I don't know about you, but when I finally made it to college, I was so excited. I'd been one of those zealous (maybe annoying) Christians for a while, so college for me was all about ministry. Everywhere I looked were new people who hadn't met Christ. My soul lit up like a bottle rocket as I got involved in every planning and praying group I could find. Bible studies, evangelism campaigns, open forums—I even started a group on comparative religion and philosophy.

Still, for one reason or another, though, nothing ever quite got me or "my people" where I expected. Stuff would start off exciting, but then nothing ever seemed to happen. I got tired and ragged pretty quickly, struggling with sin and depression like never before. Looking back, I guess most of it was about me being mad at God for holding back on me. To this day, I struggle with this recurring theme in my life: I want to glorify God and see my friends know Christ, so why isn't it happening? I do all I can and wait for God to pull through His end.

He rarely does, though.

I'm able to *say* this now, more than I actually *understand* it, but I'm learning the Christian stance is more about *being* than *doing*. In light of this, my first year struggles make more sense. God was not idle, and my efforts were not in vain. He was not concerned with the trail of accomplishments left behind, or even left undone, but with *who I was becoming* through them. God is less worried about what I do than where my motives are in doing these things. He wants me to be who I am. And who I am as a Christian is grounded in my identity in Christ.

Living this way (instead of just saying it to you) has honestly made my days a lot more enjoyable. I guess it's taken the pressure off. I don't need to be Jesus to everyone. Jesus is more than capable of that one. But I'm called to be a light to Jesus. Lights need sources, though, so returning to campus this fall, my biggest change will be *being* with my Source, instead of trying to do the sourcing myself.

A **GRINCH** NAMED MARTHA

LAFAYETTE UNIVERSITY

Courtney S.

I can say this because I am in it—college is possibly the most selfish and self-absorbed time of one's life. Almost by default, everything is always about *me* (my schedule, my job, my grades, my social life, my sleep, my dating). I was pretty involved, outreach-wise, in high school, but somehow college coerced me into my own little world. It wasn't until my social justice professor assigned ten hours of community work that I got back on track.

The first day I showed up at her nursing home, Martha Brown was the hard-hearted Grinch, who probably stole the whole year, not just Christmas. I walked in, and she *maybe* said two words to me. She was angry—old, angry, and ready to die, not even slightly concerned about a pompous college student like me.

When I returned the next week, my sole basis for returning was the free food. Honestly. That's it.

I can't say the visit did much good either, although her cracked lips edged out the words, "Thank you."

On my third visit, I decided to try a conversation (Yeah, the first two were spent staring. Sound painful? It was). I inquired about the photos on her dresser. This was the ticket. Martha went on for the next thirty minutes about her family. Her husband of thirty-three years had died of prostate cancer, and she'd lived with her son ever since. Due to financial burdens and inadequate space, Martha was forced into a nursing home and hadn't seen or heard from her family ever since.

Things began to change between us. In the following weeks, Martha slowly but surely opened up about her life history. She was one of the most brilliant, cultured, and well-traveled people I had ever met. She had encountered war, sickness, pain, and tragedy. Each successive week, layers of life were peeled back. In the second hour of our tenth week, I was convinced I'd be seeing more of Martha Brown.

I graduate this year, and, health pending, Martha will be wheeled to the front row. This woman has not only been the most influential mentor in my life, but she has also become an amazing friend. I'm sure I would have done fine living in my little enclave of college students for four years. But knowing Martha Brown made my experience whole. I realize this wholeness could've come through a variety of other outlets, but selfishly (in a good way, this time), I'm glad it was through Martha.

Sometimes I wonder, looking back, if those initial visits were really stiff and silent because of her hard heart, or mine?

I'LL BET **YOU'RE** SURROUNDED

CLEMSON UNIVERSITY

Jessica W.

My school is big and most students say they're Christians, but I'm not sure what they mean by that. For a long time I felt completely alone in my passion for God. Many nights I wanted to just chuck my faith altogether—actually, I'm surprised I didn't.

Hebrews 12:1 says: "Therefore, since we are surrounded by such a great cloud of witnesses, let us throw off everything that hinders and the sin that so easily entangles, and let us run with perseverance the race marked out for us." Surrounded by believers? I wanted to believe this, but had no reason to. I spent my first year falling and then trying to get back up on my own. I would have quiet times and maintained some elements of faith, but "maintained" was about it. I wanted to think God cared about my college years, but was seeing absolutely nothing to support that.

After a year of struggling alone, I saw a flyer for a Christian band playing on campus. Almost feeling sorry for them, I marked the calendar, knowing there were no Christians to support them

139

(and obviously no non-Christians would). I didn't even think to buy a ticket, imagining the crowd would consist of a band member's parent and maybe the campus chaplain (did we have one?).

I was wrong.

The concert had a big audience. Estimating numbers isn't my thing, but big means big. It wasn't "open your hymnal and say a quiet prayer" students, either. It was passionate Christians, Christians who worshiped God as if He was really God. I couldn't really figure out if it was for real. I felt like I had entered some reality TV show that was déjà vuing through all my dreams/frustrations/wonders from the entire last year.

I ended up meeting some great people at the concert and learning there were some other people who believed like me. I don't know if I was just too lazy, or blind, or what, that I didn't see this before that night, but getting into community has been a huge influencer in what I can now call my *growing* faith. Learn from me and don't spend an entire year of your college experience thinking you're the only serious Christian. I'm willing to bet you're "surrounded by a great cloud of witnesses," but you've got to be willing to look and ask.

CATCH A VISION

DUKE UNIVERSITY

Chris B.

I had a rude awakening last semester. I was working with a volunteer program on campus. It was basically a charter organization created to allow those with mental handicaps access to jobs. My job was venturing into the community to find organizations willing to support us. The time commitment for the businesses was one year, and they were to give the employees ten hours of work per week. Not a big deal.

The first five businesses said "no." With every receptionist, my hopes rose, but every human resource person turned us down. Excuses ranged from already having volunteer support to no room in the budget. Completely discouraged after a week of failed attempts, I had this epiphany to approach local churches—lovers of the unloved, right? So with high expectations, I set out.

Church number one: "Our hire date has expired."

Church number two: "I don't think they would be competent for the work we need done."

Church number three: "Our volunteer support is incredible and such a position isn't necessary right now."

Church number four: "I don't think that type of person could contribute to our mission statement."

Church number five: "I must admit, I think God created special job places for those types of people. But I don't think our church is one of them."

I was devastated and drove home with tears streaming down my face, completely disgusted by what the church had become. If *they* wouldn't let these people in, who would? And if we were too healthy to house the sick and sickened hearts, why did we exist? Why did Jesus come? It's rare to find a church that seeks the rejected. But isn't this our role? Isn't this why Grace stepped out of heaven? Where is the love our Savior embodied? Where is the love that seeks the unseekable and finds the lost?

I still work for this organization. In fact, I still target the churches by our campus.

A few have caught the vision, but there are many more who haven't, yet. People with mental handicaps are just that: people. They still have hearts, and they still deserve love.

I'm hopeful that college students will be among those who do catch the vision.

CAMPUS-WIDE **FLOP**

UNIVERSITY OF VERMONT

Mandy P.

I have been involved with the same campus ministry since my freshman year. At one point, I thought it would be cool to try a campus-wide event with all the ministries. I gathered with a group of friends, and we began praying about the idea. Knowing our school was diverse, we tried to incorporate a unique blend of speakers, musicians, and advertising ideas. Overall, I think we did a pretty good job. And I'm pretty realistic in knowing you shouldn't expect one event to revive God's name to an entire campus, but let me just summarize the week as whole:

Flop.

Complete, embarrassing flop.

I'm sure God worked in certain hearts that week, but in terms of sparking a campus revival, it didn't quite happen.

I think what I've realized since is that we were trying to bring lost students toward love and acceptance. But unfortunately, the organizations themselves were lost from one another. How did we expect to create cohesion in an *idea*, when we didn't have cohesion in an *identity*—as a body of believers? You could've paid me to explain the vision behind another campus

143

ministry, and I still would've had no idea. Furthermore, I realized I didn't know students from other fellowships, and our staff didn't know the staffs of other ministries.

This was a rude awakening. How were we supposed to function together on our campus if we were fighting on different teams? And maybe "fighting" is a strong word, but we certainly weren't moving as one body. I'm not saying campus ministries need to come together as one big happy family. That's naive. I am saying we represent Christ, and until we can come around that truth *together*, there's no way we'll do it apart.

A **DOER** LOOKS BACK **ON** FOUR **YEARS**

MICHIGAN STATE

Jill C.

As I sat out on our campus quad one warm April evening, reflecting on the hopes and dreams from four years behind me, I had one of those "God moments." I had read a quote from Philip Yancey earlier that morning: "There is nothing we can do to make God love us more and there is nothing we can do to make God love us less." The essence of these words should have brought me peace, but thinking about my life thus far, it brought me only regret.

Luke 10:38–42 tells the story of Christ being invited into the home of two women, Mary and Martha. Mary chose to sit at the feet of Christ, while Martha worked endlessly making preparations in their home. Distracted by all the work she was upset at Mary for leaving behind, Martha came complaining to Jesus.

"Martha, Martha," the Lord answered, "you are worried and upset about many things, but only one thing is needed. Mary has chosen what is better, and it will not be taken away from her."

I am Martha. Most days of my life, I'm the "doer." Don't hear me wrong—serving is great and I want to do it until the day I die, but I'm learning there's a call to surrender above a call to serve. It's no wonder serving often becomes more of a disservice, a heavy weight, than anything else. Done out of place, it produces negative effects for me and counterproductive outcomes for God. When I'm serving up *my* miracles, God's not really necessary. So, I'm thankful for Martha's servant heart, but I'm more thankful for Mary's surrendered one. In the fullness of our surrender, *then* I think we're really able to serve.

Chapter 8

SPORTS

P laying college sports can be incredibly joy filled. There's the camaraderie, victory, traveling, goal accomplishments. But there are also many hardships—pressure to compete, time required, mental commitment, fatigue, eating disorders…the list goes on.

As a college tennis player, my biggest struggles have been with purpose and identity. Whether you're an athlete or not, everyone wrestles with why we do what we do and who we are because of it.

People often answer the *why are we doing it* question with the Christian word that ironically turns everyone away—evangelism. I don't know how this definition got so jacked-up, but I think evangelism is simply displaying untamable love. It's that simple. Some will do it through a sport, while others through writing, singing, dancing, praying, or drawing. There's no "right" way to evangelize. You don't need to carve out sessions to talk about Jesus or plan a halftime where you'll share the gospel. You need to carve out boldness and cling to an existence where Christ is exposed—all the time. Your assignment isn't about turning people; it's about displaying a life that makes the turn worth it.

Identity is the other big issue. *Who you are* often gets defined by what you do, or how well you do it. This doesn't allow much freedom, though. Perfection is fine to pursue, but the pursuit is endless and ultimately futile, because failure along the way is guaranteed. I've found that losing sight of my identity in Christ—my "chosen, beloved, loved-as-I-am" status—leaves me in a never-ending game of losses. But when my eternal and unchangeable identity is in place, I can play hard and enjoy the game, win or lose.

—abbie

Similarly, if anyone competes as an athlete,
he does not receive the victor's crown unless he
competes according to the rules.

2 TIMOTHY 2:5

ATTITUDE

Washington and Lee University

Dwight R.

Attitude influences. I didn't learn this till college. The details don't matter anymore, but I got kicked out of a really important game my junior year because of my bad attitude. My attitude was ugly enough that day, but even uglier in days to come. And I had always been known as "the nice guy."

I guess in some ways this was a good thing. People saw that I wasn't always the perfect little Jesus guy. In a lot more ways, though, people had seen a part of me that I hate.

Paul said, "Your attitude should be the same as that of Christ Jesus" (Philippians 2:5). That's easy for me most the time, but what I'm trying to learn is how to dress myself in this attitude *all* the time, even when things don't go my way. I want Christ's jersey when I'm intentionally pushed out of bounds, God's response when the referee makes a deciding call.

I guess it's taking on a righteous attitude on good days, bad days, won games, or lost ones, so that no matter what the situation, I'm able to "rejoice and be glad in this day the Lord has made" (Psalm 118:24, paraphrased).

EIGHT HUNDRED **MILES** **OF** SELFISHNESS

GEORGIA TECH

Gordon H.

The moment I arrived on campus, my thought was, These are the stomping grounds where my dreams will be realized and my stepping stone toward life as a professional tennis player. I honestly believed I was destined to become the next Michael Chang, the foreign superstar who would surpass Andre Agassi and Andy Roddick as the next American champion.

I spent most of my adolescence in Taipei, Taiwan, and had a very successful junior tennis career. The on-court attention basically gave me my worth in life. Everything about my identity became based on my accomplishments with tennis. I was good, too, so I loved it.

Though I never felt overt pressure from my parents to "make it" per se, the underlying expectations eventually got to my head. I began to feel that if I didn't achieve what was expected of me, I'd be viewed as a failure. This vicious cycle added loads of pressure and drove me to strive to please others through high school and, unconsciously, into college. I went to school thinking it was preparation for my future professional tennis career—making academics the obvious second place.

Freshman year was fairly normal, though I didn't get the playing time I'd expected. I brushed it off as growing pains and getting used to college life. Next year I was sure to have a starting spot, and my successes could take off from there.

I became a Christian at the end of that year. My understanding was very basic, but also big enough to know that I was to yield my life to Christ's control. Jesus on the throne, not me—yet I was definitely still the ultimate king of my life. I was willing to surrender *most* aspects of my life, but couldn't get around to the tennis ones. Tennis remained the ultimate god in my life, and when it came down to it, I was still worshiping tennis, not Jesus.

Sophomore year took some turns. After a successful fall season, I injured my right foot and was forced to red shirt. By the time next fall rolled around, I was back and playing some of the best tennis of my life—constantly praising the Lord. After Christmas break, though, things went bad. Spring season started off poorly, and as my confidence dwindled, so did my faith. I thought God was abandoning me, when in reality He was just trying to get my focus back on Him. Unlike the fall, when I was able to praise God for everything, I no longer wanted to. Life got so miserable that I eventually decided to transfer.

From the start, I loved my new school! Loved the city, campus, new team...everything about it. My dreams of professional tennis had been rekindled, and it seemed the perfect place for them to unfold.

But then a funny thing happened. Five days into practice, I was hit with an overwhelming feeling that this wasn't the place for me. Five days in, somehow, I knew deep down I was supposed to be back at Georgia Tech. So believe it or not, I retransferred (not sure if that word exists). As absurd as it sounds now, I've never had a greater/weirder peace. For once, I knew God was speaking directly to me, and for once, I was actually listening.

I was fully aware that my initial transfer was purely selfish, but also that God used that eight hundred miles of selfishness to lead me to Him. I no longer felt enslaved by my performance on the tennis court. In fact, I no longer even wanted to be a famous tennis player (or maybe I just got realistic). Although the talent was clearly a blessing, His hands were in charge of its end. Though tennis remains a special part of my life, it no longer controls me.

I think the summary of what college has taught me is this: "What I once considered profit I now consider loss for the sake of Christ. What is more, I consider everything a loss compared to the surpassing greatness of knowing Christ Jesus my Lord, for whose sake I have lost all things" (Philippians 3:7–8, paraphrased).

PAID TO RUN

Samford College

Ashley G.

As a college athlete, I've encountered a lot of memorable times, but also a lot of unexpected ones. I run distance and have done it my entire life. Everyone told me running in college would be different—would be like having a job. This sounded great to me, though, as I couldn't believe I'd get paid to do what I loved (and would do anyway).

I arrived at preseason in the best shape of my life, obviously expectant of a promising fall. Things went well for a couple months, but then went downhill. Anemia, injuries, fatigue—you name it, I had it. An entire year of recurring injuries forced me to question my running career. I wanted to think God was in control, but why would He make it this way? James 1:2–4 says, "Consider it pure joy, my brothers, whenever you face trials of many kinds, because you know that the testing of your faith develops perseverance. Perseverance must finish its work so that you may be mature and complete, not lacking anything."

I wanted to be spiritual and consider my setbacks pure joy, but somehow I couldn't.

Similar to the first, my second season started off great. By October, though, fatigue and injury were back on the scene. My love for competition quickly dwindled, and the job I once thought to be so great had now become a chore. Daily, I would find myself wrestling with my role as a runner and more specifically, a runner at Samford. I finished up that season, but felt God saying "let go" after that.

This was huge for me. I wasn't a "let go" kind of girl, and since sixth grade, my life had been running. I've probably been more confused and anxious since making the decision not to run, but somehow more joyous, too. By letting go of this area of my life, I realized that I actually gained greater completion toward my role as a daughter of God, rather than as a runner. And though trials wouldn't be my first choice of a way to discover these ends, I'm discovering that they're usually well worth the challenge.

I WENT TO **COLLEGE** TO **PLAY** FOOTBALL

UNIVERSITY OF ILLINOIS

Eddie R.

Football can be a wonderful part of life. But to think football is a wonderful life gets you in trouble. I grew up to play football. I went to college to play football. Literally, I ate, slept, and lived within the sidelines of this game—junior league, middle school prep teams, state-championship high school program, and ultimately, wearing a number at the Big Ten school of my dreams. Football was my identity. It was who I was. God had never been a big part of my life. I believed in Him, but that was about it. My parents went to church, but never really cared if my brother and I went. I guess growing up in America, it's pretty hard not to be influenced by our little bubble of cultural Christianity, but for as much as I can remember, the God-thing never really held much influence on me. And if it did have an influence, it certainly wasn't positive. I started to see that my understanding of God was very "crutch"-based. It seemed pretty natural to fill my "urgent" spaces with God (exam, girlfriend, big tackle, money), but I would never think about talking to Him on a more normal basis—or what the church seems to call "a personal relationship with Jesus Christ."

To be perfectly honest, I was "using" God. Not in a bad way—I was fine with it and figured He probably was, too. Not that He was surprised by my random requests, but I just thought of Him as kind of a "Pie-in-the-sky, we'll talk when you get here" god. I knew He would listen whenever I talked, but I also assumed my little world didn't need as much attention as the president or starving kids in Africa.

It was my junior year, and football was in high gear. I was captaining the team and by midseason was high tackler. The streak didn't last for long, though. It was the fourth quarter in a home game against our biggest rival. I went in headfirst for a tackle and woke up in the emergency room. Every player's nightmare had become my hell-breathing reality. Unconsciousness was the least of my concerns, though. I'd basically crushed one leg, torn my ACL in one knee and MCL in the other, and shattered an ankle bone. I was out for a minimum of ten months and required three surgeries. Because I'd redshirted my freshman year, this meant my scholarship and football career were done. Nada. Completely finished.

The next year was spent in and out of hospitals and rehab centers, trying to regain leg strength. I was essentially *forced* to spend time with and even depend on other people. Knowing this was a bad time for me, one of the guys invited me to a ministry thing for athletes. He knew I wasn't into my faith that much, but the speaker had been a professional ball player who retired after being diagnosed with a life-threatening cancer.

I remember the speaker saying, "If God hadn't been my foundation through this disease and my inability to play football, I would be dying right now." He wasn't talking about dying in a physical sense, because from our perspective, this man was obviously dying. Yet something about his beliefs, as a Christian, was giving him life? As my friend explained later, this guy had been excused from spiritual death by accepting God's free gift of eternal life. That seemed weird...and impossible...but it also seemed pretty amazing. Even though football was a huge (and successful) part of his life, I knew that now something else had become huger.

That night was a turning point for me in a lot of ways. I'm now a second semester senior who still has lopsided legs and am a long way from full recovery. My life has changed, though. I love football and still consider it a huge part of who I am. But I also realize that it doesn't have to define me. I will never be playing pro ball and likely won't do much with the sport except watch it on TV. But I guess the bottom line is that I'm okay with that now. Football doesn't consume my identity to the point that every move I make (or don't make) labels me. God is the one who called Himself I AM, which is good, because now I don't have to be.

TEAM **BONDING**

TENNESSEE STATE

Jared P.

I came to college set on two things: 1) maintaining a solid relationship with Christ and 2) making an eternal impact on others. Both seemed fine for a while, but then soccer conditioning kicked in, and the "rushing" that goes with it got a little crazy.

I came out of high school as a four-year, all-state player and expected a starting position in college. I hate the phrase "peer pressure," but during those months, I guess that's part of what happened to me. Upperclassmen basically treated us like slaves, and "team bonding sessions" were an after-practice requirement.

I was never even forced to do anything, but I just felt pretty stupid *not* doing something. It's awful to even think about now, but I did stuff during those weeks that I'd never even thought about before. Girls, beer, property...you name it and we did it. But again, I *chose* to do these things. (This never even crossed my mind, but I wonder now what would've happened if I'd asked for another option?)

Anyway, I made the team and started all spring season.

As a third year player now, I'm still pretty embarrassed about those initial weeks of practice. Maybe *haunted* is a better word, because it just wasn't me.

People who know about this always tell me God uses all things for the good of His glory (Romans 8:28). Even crap like this? Even crap like this. I know that's true—hard to believe, but true.

I've never questioned how much He loves me after (even during) my rebellion. I know where I stand with God. Always have and hope I always will. But now I constantly ask, "How much do I love Him?" There's a song that talks about God's grace being more than enough for me. I understand that a little better now.

THE GUY WHO
KNEED ME

OLE MISS

Art D.

As athletes, our sports usually define us. As Christian athletes, our sports still usually define us. Sad but true, and unfortunately, I learned this the hard way.

It was a cloudy October morning in Oxford, Mississippi, on the second day of the Southern Collegiate Soccer League final tournament. We were down one goal to none. I was the goalkeeper and was already frustrated with the score, when hotshot number ten barreled toward me one-on-one. There was nothing in me that was going to let him score. I went down on my side, sliding hard at him like I'd done a hundred times before, but this time the forward didn't make an effort to jump over me. As he picked up his knee, it slammed into my forehead. I didn't really know what had happened with the ball; I just knew I'd been hit really hard, had a throbbing headache, and was bleeding profusely from above my left eyebrow.

Amazingly, I was fully conscious and assumed that after a little in-house ambulance treatment, I'd be in for the second half. Problems started when I got to the emergency room and the doctor said, "Here, feel this." He ran my finger across my forehead, and there was a dent about one centimeter deep with the diameter of a Ping-Pong ball. The doctor explained that my forehead was fractured, and, depending on whether it broke one or two layers of bone, there could be neurological damage. Needless to say, I was pretty scared. I'll spare the details of what followed, but the matchless point is that God used hundreds of praying people, one great doctor, twelve tiny titanium plates, and thirty-four titanium screws to heal me. Six days after surgery, I was back in class and en route to normality.

About a year later, I was studying in Mexico, and my friend Chris asked what I thought about practicing with the university squad in our city. Hesitant to play again, I agreed to practice, but not to let it get too serious. The doctor's orders were not to play at all, which I translated into playing in a very reserved manner. The main problem was that I couldn't play goalie without fearing hard contact to my head, which could lead to severe damage. So instead I played any field position available. Before, I had earned respect on the field by my abilities as goalkeeper, but now I had to play positions I honestly wasn't good at. As time passed, I saw Chris' game excel, with guys gravitating toward him and seemingly valuing him more than me, simply because he was a great player. My jealousy and rage climaxed, because I was consumed with wanting to be the hero I was accustomed to being. I wanted soccer to define who I was for those guys, instead of showing them a friendship.

Although my story obviously falls into a sports context, the fact of the matter is, whether its sports related or not, maintaining a mindful recognition of who you are in God's eyes (not the field's, player's, or scoreboard's), will make life a lot more enjoyable (and real).

Oh, and if you're wondering, the guy who kneed me did not score.

Chapter 9

GOING ABROAD

I was sitting in a coffee shop recently when a businessy-looking guy rushed in for his daily fix. He set his paper in a corner seat, proceeded to the counter, and spouted off his "medium, nonfat, no-foam latté, etc., etc., decaf" order. The barista kindly gave him his change and began making the drink. Strolling back to his plush velvet seat, the guy let a dime slip from his hand. He glanced down at it briefly, obviously decided it wasn't worth bending over for, and advanced to the counter to retrieve his drink. After a cursory scan of his paper, he was out the door.

I sat (in my plush velvet seat) pondering life in America. What has happened to our society? When did a dime merit only a disdainful glance? When did thankfulness, respect for, and enjoyment of the simplest things die? I'll never forget a Thanksgiving some years back when the entire evening passed without one mention of being thankful. America is spoiled.

Studying abroad brought this alive for me. I spent a summer in China, a semester in Paris, and short stints in Australia, Slovakia, and the Dominican Republic. I can honestly say, nothing in college changed and challenged my faith as much as these experiences. Never had I seen, heard, or lived alongside humanity in such a telling light. For the first time, God's pursuit became about all nations, not just one. All people, not just me. Studying abroad forces encounters previously left to textbooks and fosters real-life engagements formerly only seen on the six o'clock news.

This chapter isn't about convincing you to study abroad, although I'd highly recommend it. Traveling outside of America isn't the issue. Going is—going across your hall or across town can sometimes be just as transforming as going across the world. It's a chance to seek to understand someone who is "other" than you, a chance to move beyond comfortable places where following God has often become merely a habit.

There's a bigger deal going on than what you see. *Going there* won't be comfortable and will never be easy, but I guarantee it will take you places you'll never forget.

—abbie

But you will receive power when the
Holy Spirit comes on you; and you will be
my witnesses in Jerusalem, and in all Judea
and Samaria, and to the ends of the earth.

ACTS 1:8

AFRICAN SUNRISE

Auburn University

Katie G.

I thought my "quiet time" was the most important part of my day. In fact, sometimes I'm pretty sure I thought my quiet time made me a Christian. It wasn't until I studied abroad in Africa for a semester that I realized how much bigger God is than just His Word.

I didn't necessarily abandon my morning time with the Lord while overseas, but I definitely altered the *agenda* of it. I realized that instead of "being still and knowing that He is God," I had been being busy and making God who I wanted Him to be.

My first morning in Africa I sat overlooking the ocean. I saw diving dolphins and a picturesque sunrise claiming the horizon. Words, thoughts, understanding, and I daresay, all of time as I knew it, disappeared. I had never experienced God in such a culminating, vast, and majestic manner until that morning. I had never seen the depths of His eternal and sovereign power, let alone beauty, before my experience on the beach that day. God overwhelmed me by sweeping away my preconceived, innermost understandings and misconceptions. Needless to say, this was the first of hundreds of moments and experiences I was blessed with during my four months abroad.

In the past I would have been horrified to admit that I only had my "quiet time" maybe five times throughout those months. I'm far from embarrassed, however, because the amount of "quiet time" I spent coming to know and fall in love with God—with His creation, with His diverse people, with the incredible incapacity that limits our minds in fully comprehending His beauty—pales in comparison to any time I could have ever planned with God. Much of my semester was spent silent before the Lord; I was incapable of expressing anything worthy of His love for me.

Before my time in Africa, I don't think I'd ever stood quiet before the Lord—and therefore, ever truly heard His voice. Knowing God involves looking up from the pages and into His eyes. "The person fulfills his or her nature in the contemplation of God, the whole point of life." —Saint Thomas Aquinas

WHEN **IN** ROME

BAYLOR UNIVERSITY

Suzanne H.

When in Rome, do as the Romans do," right? Well, what happens if you're a Christian? What happens if you don't agree with what the Romans are doing? Much to my dismay, my pipe-dream convictions didn't match up to my experience in Rome.

The first thing our group did was get trashed on the plane ride over. Red flag number one. The only questions at orientation revolved around club and bar sites throughout the city. Flag number two. I don't mean to paint an overly critical view of my group, but it didn't take a genius to figure out my study abroad group wasn't about to hop the Jesus train. So why should I?

My first weekend in Italy taught me two things: 1) Hangovers are awful, and 2) I'd lived in a bubble (spiritually, emotionally, ethnocentrically) my entire life.

After a few more similar experiences, I gradually made it back to my prepartying standards. And I'll keep it short, because it really is short, but those standards have taken on a new dimension. Before going to Rome, my faith was really my parents' faith. My "rules" were just a textbook faith that held nothing when put against reality. And as weird as it sounds (and I wouldn't recommend it), fighting that faith and refusing those rules was really what brought me to true faith.

I had a profound realization one morning outside a flower-filled Vatican garden. If a flower is rooted well, it will continue growing to fullness. If it's fully grounded and cared for, growth is circumstantially unaffected. In a similar way, if I am grounded in my relationship with Christ, I will naturally grow and find greater desire to know Him. I'm not saying, go get drunk and you'll know Jesus; I am saying, go out into the world and ask who your God is. His scope might surprise you.

A **SUMMER** IN GALWAY

NORTHWESTERN UNIVERSITY

Grant R.

The summer after my sophomore year, I decided to study abroad with a psychology program. I just planned to have some fun traveling to interesting places and racking up course credits at the same time, but I failed to account for God's ability to work, no matter where I am.

The trip focused on the study of child development and consisted of three groups of fifteen students. My group went to Galway, Ireland, a small city on the west coast. Each group spent their first two weeks doing an intensive study of their cities' students. This consisted of just goofing off with little Irish kids and asking them questions that tested their psychological development. Our final three weeks were spent together in London, England, assembling data from each of the three sites and writing a report based on this analysis.

If I had to sum up the greatest thing I learned while abroad, it would be this: *God loves to work when we're willing to live outside our comfort zones.* Why? Because I think it's only when our circumstances bring us to a place of realizing our inadequacy that we're forced to fall on His grace.

Others on my trip were experiencing many of the same

feelings I was. I was able to dig deeper with one girl in particular, who shared her feelings of being outside of where she was comfortable. Caryn had probably gone to church about two times in her entire life, and each was an impressively negative experience. She was incredibly intellectual and one of those people who needed to analyze every possible variable to any given situation. So when I went so far as to mention the word "truth" when sharing with her my beliefs about the gospel, she couldn't settle for stopping there. Caryn asked endless questions—and we're talking deep, theological ones. Needless to say, I didn't know most of the answers, though I thankfully had some books on the trip that started her on the right track.

When she would insistently ask me questions, the only place I could turn was to my own experiences, backed by a minute knowledge of the Bible. Riding the bus to and from school together allowed us quality time to talk and share about one another's lives. Through these talks, I learned a lot about my own beliefs and was refreshed and reminded of why I believe what I do. I think being forced to talk about our faith maneuvers our beliefs to the surface, where their strength and validity can grow through testing.

Caryn loved to read, so after getting through the books I lent her, she wanted to look at the Bible. After reading Matthew, Mark, Luke, John, and Acts, she went ahead and read through the Epistles. Over a three-week span, she read two Christian books, plus most of the New Testament. This was an incredible witness to *me!* By the time our study abroad trip was over, she professed to be a Christian. God continues to work in her heart, and the crazy thing is, He was already working in her heart long before our trip.

All things are held together by God—from huge ones like the universe, solar system, and planets, all the way down to little ones like humans and all we see around us. We might as well take advantage of the holding.

FLY

Oregon State

Ian C.

S trolling beside the ocean recently, I noticed the blur of legs of a small bird on the run across the sand. I couldn't help smiling, as his feet ran full speed away from each approaching wave. Finally, the determined creature dashed one more time toward the water. And then, as if destiny were never in question, he took flight, off the sand, over the water, and into the spring air.

For some reason, the bird reminded me of my tendency to rush around, and rush around some more, trying to stay ahead of each wave in life. But I forget that in Christ, I have wings. If God's Word is true, and I really have every spiritual blessing in the heavenly realms (Ephesians 1:3), I have the power to fly, too, but more often settle for being earth-bound. I've substituted *the* victorious gift of God's power and grace for my mediocre attempts at strength.

We all want to make good and even great things happen, but we can only cover so much ground before the waves take us over. I'm wondering what would it look like to be delivered from our own feet today?

NEW STRANGER
DOWN UNDER

ELON UNIVERSITY

Bryson V.

The plane began to descend. As I peered out the window, I couldn't believe I was seeing the boundless lands of southeastern Australia. I'd left America just twenty-four hours earlier, it was late at night, and I was literally embarking upon a new world and new time in my life.

Somehow I managed to exit the airport and find a shuttle service that took me to a youth hostel. As I lay down to sleep, my mind raced with questions and concerns. How was I going to connect with people from my school? Who was going to look out for me this month before classes started? Why did I come here? Though my watch reminded me it was the middle of the night, my fears kept me awake a long time.

The next morning, I knew I needed help, but my gut/guy instinct was to avoid strangers and figure everything out on my own. Then I realized I was a stranger, too, so I might as well ask for help. Up to this point, if you were to ask me if God was a good provider, I would have easily said yes. I knew the Sunday school answers, but didn't actually *believe* them.

From that shaky beginning, good things came. Gradually, I mastered the little things like getting around, and then the bigger things like getting a roof over my head. I learned to deal with the loneliness and solitude.

Another thing: That semester reworked just about every notion I had about God. I clung to His Word, which had never been the case in America. Honestly, and I know this is gonna sound cheesy, but it was like falling in love for the first time. I'm always the guarded, hesitant guy for a while, but once I'm into you, I'm all yours (ask some of the girls I've dated). Same thing with God. As the weeks went by and I started trusting Him and even finding enjoyment in His presence, I really felt like a young boy in love.

My journey abroad revealed a new continent and culture, but also a new relationship with my Creator. I know this could've happened here just as easily, but I'm honestly glad He took me to Australia to do it. Having returned to the States and finished another semester here, it's hard to maintain that dependence in the same way—I guess because I know the ropes in America, and a lot of days, it seems like I can get through them without God.

And I guess I can, but what I want to remember from those days in Australia is that it's not nearly as fun. Life is so much more worth it when we risk depending on God.

APPOINTMENT IN SPAIN

UNIVERSITY OF VERMONT

Kate B.

Ever since I was fifteen, I wanted to live abroad in Spain. Having studied Spanish since kindergarten, I knew the only way to truly become fluent was to live in a Spanish-speaking country and be forced to think and live in the culture. In no time at all, it seemed, I was standing at the airport waiting to board my flight to Madrid. A girl from my school approached me, and we quickly realized we'd be studying in the same program.

After a long flight over, Sharon and I shared a cab to the hotel and got the scoop on each other's backgrounds/religious beliefs/etc. Sharon was raised in a Jewish household, but similar to many Americans, held many strikingly Christian beliefs. For instance, she believed that Jesus *might have been* Israel's Messiah, and when I asked her to explain this further, she didn't know how to respond. Sharon also recognized that we all have a desire for a Savior in our lives, but lacked the courage to ask herself why Christ hadn't fulfilled this role. And I specifically remember her being floored when we read through Isaiah 53 (all about the prophecy of Jesus).

As our semester progressed, I began writing out verses for

Sharon about Old Testament prophecies Jesus fulfilled in the New Testament. One of our last weekends, a group of us went dancing to celebrate our final days in Spain. When we first arrived at the bar, Sharon and I began talking about difficulties she was having with her boyfriend. This hadn't ever happened to me, but I really felt like God was asking me to share the gospel with her in light of these circumstances. I looked her straight in the eyes and said, "Sharon, Jesus is the only One who can truly satisfy you. I *know* you believe in Jesus as Savior. I know it because your eyes light up when you talk about Him. I know you believe, Sharon! Now, what's stopping you from outwardly professing that Jesus is your Savior?"

She looked back at me and said, "Nothing!"

Standing outside the bar, I asked, "Sharon, can we talk to Jesus?" She adamantly answered, "Yes." So with the black of the night covering us and the cool breeze on our backs, we stood holding hands and voiced Sharon's recognition of Jesus as Lord and Savior. I think it's funny that I went to Spain because of a childhood dream, but I also went to Spain because God wanted to unfold a bigger dream.

PURE AND **SIMPLE** IN **CHINA**

DUKE UNIVERSITY

Jen G.

G rowing up in the South, I viewed Christianity as a belief system with no consistency. One church preached one thing, while the same denomination across the street would preach another. For some, Christianity was ritual; for others, it was the Bible. For one family, it was prayer; for another, service. In short, America makes Christianity look like a confusing, contradictory, and impossible-to-understand concept. I think this is why so many people hate the church. And I might even say, rightly so.

When I went abroad to China, I still hadn't grasped a unified perspective of who the God of the Bible really was. But as I sat in a delicately sculptured teahouse with my nonbelieving Chinese friend, she explained it to me. I shared everything I knew about God, and then she shared every desire she had about wanting Him—wanting Him as Father, friend, "benevolent Savior" (I loved that). The only word that comes close to explaining her grasp of an eternal message—shared in less than an hour—was *pure*. A word absent from my Christian vocabulary. Ada's decision to put her faith in Jesus Christ was innocent and unadulterated.

She got it—maybe more than I got in so many ways.

Ada had a basic comprehension that she was a sinner and Christ had to, but also *chose* to, shed blood on her behalf. Knowing this story isn't exactly fairy-tale status, I figured the people of China would like the drama, but write it off as "American." My notions were so watered-down that the miracle of God's Word being "living and active, sharper than any double-edged sword and penetrating even to the dividing soul and spirit, joints and marrow, judging attitudes of the heart" (Hebrews 4:12) was sadly overlooked.

In China, there are no radical splits between denominations. The need for denominations, at all, has yet to catch hold. There are no street preachers and no manger scenes diluted with tacky lights. In essence, there are few preconceived notions jading the life of Christ. For them, understanding God is based on Scripture and personal testimonies. Period. The gospel basics that we speed by on billboards and paste onto bumper stickers are compelling for them. The concept of being separated from a Creator, died for by a Savior, and reconnected through faith in His resurrection, is enough. More than enough.

I realized a lot that afternoon. For one thing, Ada taught me how inconsistent my faith is. It's like an ocean, empowered by rushing waters at one point, and crashing into depths of sand at another. Instead of allowing the purity and even simplicity of the gospel to sustain my foundations, I'd allowed "bubblegum" Bible studies and even American presentations of the church itself to define my Christianity. My prayer returning is that purity would chip away at these fringes. We may not be called to an easy message, but we're definitely called to a simple one. I want to live it that way.

Chapter 10

BARRIERS

Racial misunderstandings and tensions remain an enormous problem in this country. And that includes on college and university campuses. From conflicts between roommates, student groups, or political organizations, ethnic barriers pop up everywhere. The easier response is denying, minimizing, or simply "managing" the problem. But the harder, better choice is addressing it. Jesus wasn't a peacekeeper. He was a peacemaker.

Being a white American doesn't lend me much credit on this issue. I'm well aware that experientially, I lack empathy for what people have lived and died for. So, I will leave you to the words of friends who fight these battles on a day-to-day basis. I will also leave you to the timeless words of God.

—abbie

For he himself is our peace, who has made the two one and has destroyed the barrier, the dividing wall of hostility, by abolishing in his flesh the law with its commandments and regulations. His purpose was to create in himself one new man out of the two, thus making peace, and in this one body to reconcile both of them to God through the cross, by which he put to death their hostility. He came and preached peace to you who were far away and peace to those who were near. For through him we both have access to the Father by one Spirit. Consequently, you are no longer foreigners and aliens, but fellow citizens with God's people and members of God's household, built on the foundation of the apostles and prophets, with Christ Jesus himself as the chief cornerstone. In him the whole building is joined together and rises to become a hold temple in the Lord. And in him you too are being built together to become a dwelling in which God lives by his Spirit.

EPHESIANS 2:14–22

A **COMMON** LANGUAGE

Emory University

Antonette S. and Veronica C.

Antonette is a black woman. Veronica is a white woman. They were placed in the same small group during their freshman year at Emory University. An interview follows:

What was your first impression of being in a group with all whites (or with a black person)?

Antonette: On first thought I would have said that being in an all-white group never really felt awkward, because I didn't grow up in a segregated environment. But just because you're accustomed to a certain environment, doesn't mean others are. Honestly, I usually only feel my skin color when I feel like others are aware of it. And not that the other girls in my group were blatant about the fact that I was the only black person, and they were all white. It's just that there is always tension in the way things are done. It's not out of one group being obnoxious to another. A lot of it is just exposure (or lack thereof) to a culture where they think, act, or speak differently. I guess it's always a little weird at first, because you're looking or hoping for that one person to connect with in any new group. They may not have to be of your same race, but oftentimes that's the first level

181

of connection—appearance. I have a lot of black friends, but I have a lot of white friends, too. Differences are not a bad thing. They identify us.

Veronica: When I arrived at our first small group meeting, I immediately noticed Antonette. I don't think of myself as prejudiced, but I was definitely surprised to see a black girl in the group. I remember feeling ashamed at the time and am still embarrassed for expecting our small group to be all white. My first thoughts were that we weren't going to have a lot in common. I didn't put up a wall or look down on her; I was just mentally preparing myself that I may not be able to relate to Antonette as well as the others. I tried to have an open mind, but for some reason part of my heart remained hesitant. At my church back home, we never had small groups that mixed various races. It seemed like all the races were lobbying for equality and in doing so, were always forming their own elite groups. It felt like we were all coexisting in our own separate worlds.

What presuppositions did having someone of another race create, in terms of your hopes for the group?

Antonette: Because I didn't allow myself to focus on the fact that I was the only black in the group, I didn't feel uncomfortable being in public and just hanging out with any of the girls. But I did realize early on that there were some things that differed and might never be understood in a group of whites, as it would in a group of blacks. I'm not saying that my group would never understand my humor or history or way of conversing, but there's just a certain comfort level that happens naturally when relating to my black friends.

Veronica: When I pictured our small group, I imagined a

group of girls so close-knit that we shared our most intimate secrets with one another. But because of my own hesitations in getting to know Antonette, my ideas of closeness seemed to fade a bit. I still desired, however, to learn how to love this girl and try to relate to her as best I could.

What have you been most challenged by in knowing each other?

Antonette: If by "challenged," you mean difficulty getting to know Veronica because of racial differences, then there were honestly no challenges right off. I just looked at her as a friend and really didn't see any challenges in the fact that we were two different races. But there are always certain aspects of your life that need more explanation—for example, little things like the differences in our hair, the environment of our churches, the way people look at us in society. Some things I've done or people I'm in contact with are completely different for her. It's just a way of life. And if the person is willing to listen and learn, then there's no reason to get upset.

If anything, the biggest "challenge" for me has been sharing prayer requests for the economic hardships of my family. I don't like to make assumptions, but most whites that attend Emory come from families that have financial stability, and for some reason it's really hard for me to relay these personal requests. I know this is bad, but I almost feel like I'm inferior in some way, because of how society portrays success. And because I'm so closed about the matter, I don't know if Veronica's ever really "suffered" financially before. And I'm not saying that all blacks are poor, or even that I'm necessarily poor, but the way our country has been founded, blacks have almost been forced to remain a culturally poor race. There are definitely exceptions, but in the grand scheme, economics seem to show the least amount of equality. Knowing and being constantly aware of that, even if I had a black friend who was well off, I would still feel more comfortable, because I'd know there was probably some struggle for her parents or someone else, to get them where they are. But again, pride is a dangerous thing and will make you believe lies that don't exist.

Veronica: I don't think *challenged* is quite the word I'd use. Blessed is more like it. It has been amazing to see my immaturity in understanding racial relations. Although I have never been "prejudiced" in terms of viewing one culture as superior to another, my heart has always assumed other races wouldn't understand me as well as my own. God has radically broken that assumption for me.

What have you been most amazed by in your relationship with Veronica (or Antonette)?

Antonette: I can now reach a comfort zone with Veronica. I don't feel inferior. She doesn't think differently when I tell her about my financial situation, but whether financial or not, there's space to encourage now. We trust enough to put everything on the table, and that's when God seems to really work. I guess that's when we give Him *permission* to. Veronica is not just "one of my white friends"; she's my friend.

Veronica: I have been overwhelmed doing morning Bible studies with her. Her heart is way cooler than mine. Antonette's fervent love for God helps me understand God's fervent love for all people.

How has your friendship with each other changed your perspective of God?

Antonette: Veronica has been such an encouragement to me. Her friendship has proven to me even more that God is a big God. He doesn't want us to limit our relationships to what's comfortable. He wants to spread it. Our friendship is a witness to others, because they see that we are not tied down by skin color. Despite our physical differences, we are sisters in Christ.

Veronica: My relationship with Antonette has shown me that God is not a god of confusion. Even though my life may be completely different from a young girl in China, or a woman in Russia, God speaks the same language. Although we come from completely different families, experiences, even church backgrounds, we share our cornerstone in Jesus Christ.

How do you foresee this friendship influencing your life and views of other races in the future?

Antonette: This friendship will further confirm that friendship knows no limits. This is not my first nonblack friendship, and it will not be my last. I like making friends outside of my race, because there is so much more you can learn about yourself from others. And there is that much more of a chance to break down walls and barriers that might have previously existed. The reassurance that everyone struggles and everyone has his or her fear and weaknesses is something I often forget.

Veronica: I think it has allowed me to be more transparent with people of other races. My friendship with Antonette is a gift, and I'm glad my own ignorance didn't cause me to miss out. I think I'll be more open and honest now, realizing that God alone has the power to knit His people together. In knowing we are all one body, I hope to be more mindful of unity.

DIFFERENCES

UNIVERSITY OF CHICAGO

Christina C.

I am not a racist. I have diverse friends. The color of a person's skin does not matter to me..."

I wish these statements were true.

No, actually, I don't wish the latter were true. For some fantastically brilliant reason, God didn't make us all colorblind. Our skin tones, nose shapes, eye curves, and hair colors confirm that we are fearfully and wonderfully made—which means that every mole, every bone, every dimple, was intentionally and purposefully designed. (Our looks are merely a glimpse of His abounding creativity!)

I used to think race shouldn't be a highlighted issue. Perhaps it was my own insecurity of not wanting to address the fact that I am a Chinese American. Perhaps I wanted to be seen as different in my own fabricated way, not the way I was created. Perhaps I knew that if I humbled myself to look to Him for answers, He would pick apart my comfortable and makeshift faith.

But we must care, not so we look like a happy, colorful family, but so we meet God at the heart of the issue. Disregarding race and culture disregards His creation. Understanding race and differences begins a journey to awe and wonder—who is He, this King of Glory? Then, when that magnificent day occurs, we will be prepared to bow down and worship our King with every nation, tribe, people, and language.

MIXING COLORS

MISSOURI STATE

Lauren K.

I confess that I'm writing this from a middle-class, Caucasian perspective, therefore immediately robbing me of much empathy for a topic like racism. Honestly, I can remember no instance in college, much less my lifetime, when the color of my skin (with the exception of freckles maybe), affected the way I was treated. At the same time, however, I have seen the direct impact and destruction the issue continues to create. Racial separation and even segregation remains a huge problem on campuses across this nation. And Christian organizations are no stranger to them.

If anyone were going to attempt unifying races, wouldn't it seem a task fit for the Christians? Shouldn't we be the ones who love our neighbors above ourselves and treat one another as sisters and brothers in Christ? Funny then, that our groups seem the most exclusive of any. Why? It's bad enough to have denominations, but why are there separate black, white, Korean, and Chinese churches of the same denomination—sometimes at the same intersection?

Nature makes us creatures of habit and certainly those who migrate toward likeness. But what about the unnatural newness we share in common as a gift from God? We're supposedly "united with Christ" and "will make his joy complete by being like-minded, having the same love, being one in spirit and purpose" (Philippians 2:1–2). I've not seen that one in my church pews.

I don't know where you fall in this discussion, but I do know one thing: God doesn't work through one ethnicity or cater to one people group. Therefore, it's naive and frankly, boring, to think a singularly faceted, exclusive color would impact a campus. Is unity practical? Hardly. But is it possible? Absolutely! Pressures against unity will not change. The capacity to overcome them, however, won't either. Jesus died for it two thousand years ago.

Being a Christian isn't about stamping sameness, but about discovering, honoring, and celebrating uniqueness.

BIRACIAL ME

SOUTHERN METHODIST UNIVERSITY

Carly B.

B eing biracial means each of your parents comes from a different ethnic background. The beauty of this word and concept, *biracial,* is that it can incorporate any ethnic group in unison. There is a misconception that there are many different skin colors, when in fact, there is only one: melanin. Having little melanin makes us light skinned, and having more melanin makes us darker skinned. The natural conclusion is that people of varying melanin levels will produce unique off-spring. The biracial issue comes in when the melanin levels are completely different.

Anyway, anatomy aside, my hope in this reflection is to simply address the core struggles that my being biracial causes on a daily basis. The United States is far from cleansed from the hate-filled history that took place before, during, and after our nation's Civil War. Today, the outward remains of that hatred are manifested as an inward, dichotomous mindset. To this day in the United States, there are literally no two ethnic groups more separate than blacks and whites.

Several biracial people have spoken out, either directly or indirectly, communicating their sole identity with being black.

Now, please understand that I truly celebrate this choice. I honestly feel that it is their God-given right to choose how they want to identify themselves, but here is the problem: I don't identify myself that way. If there were ever a specially defined biracial ethnicity, I would claim that, for I do not claim to be black or white—but both.

I was born in Kansas, raised in Florida, and attend college in Texas. I attended a predominantly white elementary school, but my middle school had a better blend of ethnicities; high school was mainly black, and now college is back to white. I am a member of a "black" church, yet very involved with a "white" campus fellowship. One of my roommates is black. The other two are white, and on the guy front, I'm really impartial. All this to say, I've lived the spectrum.

Being biracial is often confusing. It seems a consistent paradox that when my fellowship in either a predominantly white or black group begins to grow, increased feelings of unbelonging in either tend to creep up. The most difficult emotional struggle is being part of both groups, but not *truly* part of either. For a while I felt like my effort to celebrate both heritages left me more isolated than anything else, yet somehow I still want to celebrate both. I guess I've realized the healthiest way to approach my biracial identity is seeking friendships with both blacks and whites. I don't mean fulfilling some sort of racial quota, but I do mean being intentional toward a full investment of both my halves.

THE RACISM VIRUS

GORDON COLLEGE

Josh T.

R acism infuriates me. I didn't grow up in an environment where blacks and whites were treated differently; rather, the racism I learned was specific to Hispanics and Filipinos. Growing up in southern California, I thought diversity was fine and good—even normal—at least until it invaded the supremacy of whites. Now, the remaining threads of racism in our nation often fascinate and disgust me.

More profoundly, however, is the way the church, in many ways, fuels this racism. How is this possible? How can the ignorance of Christians be so harmful, yet I remain proud to call myself a follower of Christ? Or am I?

Recently, God has been teaching me about the need for the church in our society. Prior to this, I was determined that Christ could more easily reveal His truth without the church and its hypocrisy. He doesn't need a group of people who claim one thing on Sunday, yet practice another throughout the week—let alone a group of professed followers who rarely own up to sinning. Here's the bottom line—Christ doesn't *need* us to accomplish ends. But He's *chosen* us. Big difference.

Racism is clearly a sin. This doesn't need verification by a

Scripture or sermon. The pain it causes is proof enough. But something I struggle with is why so few people seem pierced by this sin?

Today I think about my campus, and even body of fellowship, and realize the amount of racism therein. There must be a greater cause, a larger power, and a better reason. It is grace alone that leads my broken heart to repentance. Racism is a deadly virus that continues injecting diseases on campuses and campus ministries nationwide. We must stop it.

PINK BLOBS, WHATEVER BLOBS

University of North Florida

Melissa M.

N adia was the nicest cafeteria lady I'd ever met. Never a day in my first two years at the dining hall did her stunning Ethiopian grin not greet me with pleasure. We would rarely talk about more than weekend plans or an upcoming test and occasionally, our respective churches. Though she never over-did it, Nadia would often express how much she wanted me to visit her church.

After a year of telling her no, I finally decided to take up the offer.

The entire congregation was Ethiopian. I've been to a lot of churches, but this was different. First off, it was four hours long—more time than I'd spend doing just about anything. Plus, everything was different...the music, the building, the people, the procession, the pastor, the language...everything. But I guess my biggest take-away was realizing my faith—my rituals, church, assumptions, expectations, even means to God—does not define *the way*. It is not *the truth*, and it is not *the life*.

As much as I hated to admit, everything in me wanted to rise up that morning and declare, "This is wrong!" or, "Fine for you guys, but when you want the real deal, come to my church."

Nadia's church didn't match my mold, but her faith sought the same God mine did. Her heart claims the same Love mine does. Seems sad that we've let God's creativity become a stumbling block to His full-bodied masterpiece. We distort it into blobs. Single-hued, separate blobs. Pink blobs. Mahogany blobs. Whatever blobs.

What a sad loss, when a canvas of so many colors is possible. And waiting.

Chapter 11

SMALL **MOMENTS**

I t was a Friday afternoon during my sophomore year. A group of us were hanging out after class and talking about weekend plans. After everyone shared their exciting agendas, the conversation turned to me. I knew perfectly well what I was doing, but was completely embarrassed to say it. I think my final wording came out, "I, uhhh...I'm going on some retreat-like thing with a bunch of friends." Feeling the blush rise to my cheeks, I diverted to another topic.

Yes, it was a retreat, and yes, it was with a bunch of friends, but it was also an evangelism training conference (which I obviously needed) with the Christian campus fellowship I was involved in.

Walking back to the dorms, a guy from the conversation approached me and asked, "Does that retreat happen to be for Christians?"

"Yes," I was now able to respond confidently, "it actually is. Are you going?"

"No, but I had no idea there were other Christians on this campus, let alone a Christian organization that would plan a retreat."

Thank God for the courage of some Christians. This guy not only attended the retreat, but now serves consistently in a campus ministry. He was my walking reminder to: "Be strong and courageous. Do not be terrified; do not be discouraged, for the LORD your God will be with you wherever you go" (Joshua 1:9).

God's will *will* prevail, regardless. Regardless of your intentions, expectations, or efforts, He is in control of your days—not you. He is the one waking the dawn and holding the stars. Don't be too busy to see it or too bashful to talk about His beauty in the smallest of moments. You never know who might be listening.

—abbie

"This is the day the LORD has made;
let us rejoice and be glad in it."

PSALM 118:24

I DON'T UNDERSTAND

UNIVERSITY OF MINNESOTA

Jake B.

People in their twenties don't get cancer. Or at least they're not supposed to. In the space of a few sentences recently, I found out my friend has a brain tumor. He's twenty-two.

Soon after telling me his bad news, my friend told me something: "I don't understand this. I don't understand the pain, the prognosis, the reason, or even the reality. But what I do understand is that not for a moment would I take back what I've been given. Not for a moment would I consider this a regret."

I don't understand that. How could he not consider this regretful? Regretfully evil, even?

He has a bigger faith than me. Clearly our circumstances vary, but as I reconsider my life, I can't say it's "regretless."

Job told us that God gives and takes away, which might not be fair, but it's true. The choice I have is choosing this truth over fairness. God does not need my approval or understanding for Him to be God. He claims to love us jealously, but freely allows us to choose to love others more than Him. God heals, but is willing—apparently—to wound me in the name of grace.

I'm trying to understand that one, too.

As a student in a regret-filled world, I'm trying to focus

more on the *process* of God today—not the destination, but the journey. As my faithful brother would joyfully attest, that journey is marked at every step by God's forbearance, by His good will.

In the meantime, it's hard to look at my twenty-two-year-old friend with cancer and say I don't regret it.

WAFFLE HOUSE
CHURCH

UNIVERSITY OF CALIFORNIA, BERKELEY

Brian F.

L ast week I had a syrup-soaked spiritual awakening. I was just finishing up an afternoon breakfast when my yellow-hued frustrations collided with a God-renewed vision. The diner walls showed no religious art of any kind. There was no high ritual. But in a matter of moments, the skies opened up, and revelation crashed in. Suddenly, I saw it—culture's newest cathedral, Christ's modern church...

Waffle House.

To my left was the soccer mom, distracted by two kids and centerpieced by a cell phone, on which a third child was likely requesting to be picked up. To my right was the intellect, exam preparation of some sort under way, with articles galore and Sweet'N Low scraps spreading over the table. Crowding the corner were the infamous "adolescents," dressed to the grunge nines. Plus Marlboros, of course. A guy in the other corner was hard to read. He sat alone, but somehow appeared content. No book, no conversation. Just *there*. Odd. Intriguing. Anyway, my favorite was the couple by the jukebox. Had to be in their eighties, but laughed and loved like euphoric eighteen year olds.

Caught off guard by this Waffle House "moment," I wondered why I'd been struck so hard by it. What about it pointed me to Christ? And then it hit me.

This Waffle House seemed like a well-drawn blueprint of the church—or at least the "meant-to-be" church. It was a picture of diversity, a collection of strangers, all brought here for one intense reason. These congregants didn't come because they felt guilty, or out of habit (as far as I knew, anyway). They came because they were hungry. They came to be filled at "America's place to work and America's place to eat."

Waffle House actually started as the dream of two neighbors who wanted something that focused on people, while serving quality food at great value (I'm not making this up—see www.wafflehouse.com).

If you think about it, our college years are all about dreams, about potential, about the future. Of course, God doesn't need another college student to change His world, and He certainly doesn't need a new Waffle House. But if Jesus and Waffle House could ever meet, the Waffle House Church would change the world.

SOMETIMES I IMAGINE GOD

JAMES MADISON UNIVERSITY

Casey S.

Sometimes I imagine God as a saintly old man, sitting on some golden throne, or maybe full-size rocking chair, answering prayers and keeping the world on its axis. I think that's wrong, though. God invented creativity and is the leader of ingenuity and progression. Why do I think He's old and out-dated? Try to explain the intricacy of a flower. Can't. Attempt to describe the making of a sunrise. Impossible. Childbirth? Miracle. Brain—can't explain. Heaven—unreal. Hell? No idea, but maybe more real than the others. You get the point. Life is an endless journey of learning, and to say otherwise sells God short. Never let me say I "get God" or "understand His ways." They are infinitely higher than mine! God is not a wallflower or a "let's stay at home and pray" monk (I'm not cracking solitude, or monks, just making a point). He *makes* peace, doesn't *keep* it. Pursues hearts, doesn't pick at them. He understands us. Sympathizes. Empathizes…"For we do not have a high priest who is unable to sympathize with our weaknesses, but we have one who has been tempted in every way, just as we are—yet was without sin. Let us then approach the throne of grace with confidence, so that we may receive mercy and find grace to help us in our time of need" (Hebrews 4:15–16). This implies that we'll be tempted. College may be the worst, but Jesus cares. He's concerned, but not overwhelmed. He's adamant about helping, but not ashamed. He gladly turns our way and never turns His back. He didn't call us to be sinless because He knows we're not capable. He sent Himself, though, and hopes we'll latch on. In Christ, we're full. Fully alive and fully living.

That's all. I just wanted to talk about God for a minute.

LEAPING INTO MANHOOD

ELON UNIVERSITY

Bryson V.

There I was, standing at the edge of a cliff, darkness surrounding me and my knees wobbling with fear. It was a warm summer night, yet my toes felt cold on the wet rocks supporting my nearly naked body. Uneasiness swept through my mind. I'm not usually the one to follow someone else's lead, but in this case I would follow just about anyone...off that cliff and into the water far below.

I'd been studying with these men for the entire year. We were on an intentional pursuit to discover our wild and adventurous manhood. It was what I'd been longing for, but also what I'd continued to fight against. I was sick of suburban living, sick of being trapped into concrete molds and measured directions. I was tired of distractions and weary of façades. At the deepest levels, I was tired of suppressing deeply felt values and important passions.

So, standing atop that cliff, afraid of my jump into the abyss, I was also looking forward to diving deeper into life than I ever had before. There was something like a fierce lion roaring from the depths of my soul, and it was time to let him out.

So I jumped.

I'll never forget falling silently through the darkness and finally hitting the water…and sinking down, down. Then I floated up to take my first breath as a new man.

As I talked with the guys later that night (post-jump!), we all felt we'd been offered a fresh shot at manhood: not something to be exalted, but hopefully to be embraced. Something about the jump gave me a new sense of being free and wild, not in a chauvinist, psycho way, but in a deeply sensed *me* way.

That leap off the edge and into the night was a rite of passage. I passed from what was known and safe to what was new and unknown, but necessary. On the way down, I heard my heart for maybe the first time. It was alive and free, and it was screaming.

Chapter 12

A FAITH **WORTH** **MORE** THAN GOLD

A s far as I know, no one has made it out of life alive. For some reason, though, we live as if we will be the first. In college especially, no one seems concerned about life's passing frailty. But if we can all agree that this life will end, shouldn't we ask, What won't?

God's answer is to look beyond what we *can* see, into a hope of what we cannot (Hebrews 11:1, paraphrased). This is faith, and this is truly living.

That being the case, keeping, nurturing, and sharing our faith is not just the business of our college years, but of our whole lives on earth. So, yes, we *can* keep our faith—and in doing so, expect to gain a lot more!

Culture will tell you that college and a passionate devotion to Jesus are mutually exclusive. But the truth is much different, as I hope you've seen in these pages. The fact is, an intense campus experience and an intense Jesus experience can combine into a powerful, positive force that will shape the rest of your life. Jesus changed the world in a ministry span of three years. Don't doubt He can do it again.

We're all on a journey of becoming—not there yet, but not content to just stay here, either. It's okay not to have Jesus, college, or the mix of the two figured out. The journey of becoming is about being with God—being and becoming more passionately His.

God brought you to a campus—or is in the process of bringing you to one—for a good purpose, and one only you can walk out. Love Him desperately. Live in Him daily—because your faith, as the apostle Peter writes (see below), has truth and life and hope written all over it—and it's "of greater worth than gold."

—*abbie*

Praise be to the God and Father of our Lord Jesus Christ!
In his great mercy he has give us new birth into a living
hope through the resurrection of Jesus Christ from the dead,
and into an inheritance that can never perish, spoil or fade—
kept in heaven for you, who through faith are shielded by
God's power until the coming of the salvation that is ready
to be revealed in the last time. In this you great rejoice,
though now for a little while you may have had to suffer grief
in all kinds of trials. These have come so that your faith—
of greater worth than gold, which perishes even though refined
by fire—may be proved genuine and may result in praise,
glory and honor when Jesus Christ is revealed. Though you
have not seen him, you love him; and even though you do not
see him now, you believe in him and are filled with an
inexpressible and glorious joy, for you are receiving the
goal of your faith, the salvation of your souls.

1 PETER 1:3–9